Robert W Sloan

The Great Contest

The chief advocates of anti-Mormon measures reviewed by their speeches

in the House of representatives, January 12, 1887, on the bill reported by

J. Randolph Tucker as a substitute for Senator Edmund's bill against the

Mormon church

Robert W Sloan

The Great Contest
The chief advocates of anti-Mormon measures reviewed by their speeches in the
House of representatives, January 12, 1887, on the bill reported by J. Randolph
Tucker as a substitute for Senator Edmund's bill against the Mormon church

ISBN/EAN: 9783337297893

Printed in Europe, USA, Canada, Australia, Japan

Cover: Foto ©Lupo / pixelio.de

More available books at **www.hansebooks.com**

THE
Great ✦ Contest.

The Chief Advocates of Anti-Mormon
Measures

REVIEWED

*By their Speeches in the House of Representatives, January
12, 1887, on the Bill Reported by J. Randolph
Tucker as a Substitute for Senator
Edmund's Bill against the
Mormon Church.*

BY R. W. SLOAN.

Salt Lake City, Utah:

1887.

AN EXPLANATION.

As THIS pamphlet is mainly a review of speeches, the immediate interest in which is past, and regarding a bill partially law and partially destroyed, it may be thought an attempt is making to revive a dead issue, to re-fight a battle that is over. There is one solid reason against such a thought: In all times the same charges are forever being made against Mormons and their faith. Though constantly denied, and persistently proven untrue, they are still repeated, and it is not unlikely that they will continue to be. The design in this work is to prove that these statements, thus made, and coming ever from one general source, must be false, because inherently contradictory; and being contradictory, they are valueless and discredit the source. If this can be done, and I am sure it is possible, something of perennial value to the cause of truth will have been accomplished. The reader must judge to what extent the object has been attained; how far it fails of being reached. But the subject itself is not a dead issue, and will never be uninteresting so long as there is opposition to the work of truth. There is no other excuse to be offered for this pamphlet.

CONTENTS.

CHAPTER I.

CHAPTER II.

CHAPTER III.

CHAPTER IV.

CHAPTER V.

CHAPTER VI.

CHAPTER VII.

CHAPTER VIII.

CHAPTER IX.

THE GREAT CONTEST.

*Speeches of the Chief Advocates of Anti-Mormon
Measures Reviewed.*

CHAPTER I.

FIGHTING FOR HUMAN LIBERTY.—A COMPARISON: MORMONS
AND EARLY CHRISTIANS.—WHY CHRISTIANITY SURVIVED.
—A POLITICAL TRICK.—POLYGAMY A TRIFLING CONCERN.
—A "LOYAL" LEAGUE.—HOW IT WAS WORKED.—WHY.—
PAP WANTED ALL ROUND.—YOUNG MORMONS THE HOPE.
—PAST AND FUTURE, FROM THE SUMMIT OF FIFTY YEARS.
—A FRAGMENT OF HISTORY.—THE LIGHT OF PROPHECY.
—THE TRUST OF MORMONS.—GOD AND THE CONSTITU-
TION.

IT has been the claim of the Latter-day Saints that in
making a defense in their own behalf they have been
fighting for liberty in behalf of all men. At first blush this
claim seems presumptuous. But if it be examined closely
there will be found much to justify the assumption. Not that
they have courted the assaults made upon them; but as a
pecularity of their history, no action against them, either
by lawless mobs or through legal means, has ever been taken
that was not in violation of some principle dear to every liberty-
loving heart. Thus, in defending themselves, they have stood
manfully for principles that must endure forever, and which,
violated even as a temporary expedient, or in response to "the
tyrant's devilish plea"—necessity—bring unerring retribution
when turned from their natural purpose. A philosopher
declares that "it is *never* sensible to *permit* what is bad for
the supposed sake of preventing what is worse;" and it has
been the fate of all those who have undertaken the solution
of this so-called problem, that they have been compelled to

2

stifle many reproofs of a better judgment in the wild hope that out of temporary harm ultimate good might come. Such a hope is in the face of all reason, as it is against all experience. This has been the great difficulty in the way of "eradicating" Mormonism. It is because of this phase that Mormonism has become known as a "vexed problem;" because of this also that men possessed of instinctive statesmanship have never touched the problem. But we do find those of vulpine sagacity—ambitious, with intellects proportioned to the sagacity that is the inherent instinct of the vulpine —madly protesting, despite the experience of all times, temporary evil to be justifiable that worse may not survive, and that such a departure from good will be in the cause of good. Reduce the proposition to a simple form and test it. When that which is wholly good brings forth that which is bad, then the wholly bad may produce good. Not till then; and this will never be. Yet it was on this plea—a temporary evil in behalf of permanent good—that the advocates of this policy urged the adoption of measures against the Mormons by the last Congress.

Another great obstacle with those endeavoring to solve the Mormon problem is that the solution could only be accomplished by the destruction of the Mormon Church. No one dare advocate this as a general principle. The instinct of self-preservation in every sane man would revolt at such an attempt. Because of this, efforts have been made to cast obloquy upon the people, that the nation might esteem the alleged evils designed to be eradicated but the outgrowth of license, as distinguished from religion. The great cry has been polygamy. Read the speeches of the three representatives in favor of this bill in the House on January, 12, 1887, and while it will be seen that the ostensible object in view was to suppress polygamy, each speaker in behalf of the bill stated distinctly that the purpose of the act was more. Mr. Taylor declared that the bill "contemplated more than the suppression of polygamy," and Mr. Tucker that polygamy was only "an incident," "a very small part of the whole business." A Church, because of the political strength of its members, was to be destroyed. The principle of religious freedom, the right of worship—a constitutional right—was at stake. No man has ever dared put the issue in this light, and yet advocate such methods. But men have clothed themselves in false armor and under the cry of "polygamy" made an assault on a principle, believing—sincerely many, but madly all—that the end would justify the means. There is a most striking parallel between the character given the Mormons to-day, and that given the early Christians (adored in this age) who were sawn asunder, crucified, burned at the stake in Roman gardens as torches, and given to satisfy the hunger of wild beasts by pagan Romans and idolatrous Jews, for precisely the same reasons that are now urged as justifying the methods adopted against Mormons, viz: because they and their religious customs were a menace to good government. One writer, speaking of the view the Romans held of early Christians, makes use of this language: "They confused them with the whole, degraded mass of Egyptians and Oriental impostors and brute worshipers; they disdained them as seditious, turbulent, obstinate and avaricious; they regarded them as mainly composed of the very meanest slaves out of the gross and abject multitude; their proselytism they considered as the clandestine initiation into some strange and revolting mystery, which involved, as its direct teachings, contempt of the gods, and the negation of all patriotism and all family affection; * * * they thought it natural that none but the vilest slaves and silliest women should adopt so misanthropic and degraded a superstition; they characterized their customs as 'absurd, sordid, foul and depraved,' and their nation as prone to superstition, opposed to religion!" Suetonious and Tacitus speak of the early Christian religion as a "new," "pernicious," "detestable," "execrable" superstition. Were I to read the above language, not knowing its application, I should solemnly aver it to be a reference to the Mormon people of to-day—an expression of the views entertained toward them by so-called Christians.

The early Christian faith was sought to be destroyed. The effort failed. It did not fail, however, because the early Christians were perfect. It failed because the Romans, in this as they had for a long period in other regards, sought to destroy that which they esteemed evil by doing wrong themselves. Not more surely does nature punish those who violate her laws, than do moral laws inflict penalties upon transgressors—and the one in the main is as little concerned about the good intentions of the wrongdoer as the other. The Christian religion survived and the vile and unredeemed paganism of Rome fell—not because men and women were burned at the stake, mutilated, and, living, turned in to be devoured by wild beasts, but because the Christian faith could not be assaulted save by transgressing principles which were true, and just, and eternal. The parallel is perfect. I cite but one case out of thousands. History of this kind makes no mistakes. It always produces the same results under the same conditions. It is not a phenomenon. It is an immutable law.

If the argument of the enemies of Mormonism were based on polygamy alone, there might be some justification—though a lame one; but the very instant they leave that, not a single point is raised against Mormons that cannot also be turned against every other church with equal force. Therefore, in defending their own church rights Mormons defend the principle by which every church enjoys freedom of worship, freedom to control its own concerns and to propagate its doctrines. When the law viciously attacks a Mormon because of his belief, and he resents, he then fights not only for his personal rights, but he defends, (and he cannot help it) that principle by which every member of every denomination, the believer in every creed, the very infidel and the atheist, enjoy the eternal right to hold their own judgment in all life's concerns without let, or hindrance, or scorn, or deprivation of rights by any man in all the world—by all men in all the earth.

Mr. Tucker declares:

"When religion veils itself in mystery and organizes its power over its individual members under the dread claim of a Divine commission to direct the actions and bind the consciences of men—when it accumulates great wealth, and thus, through superstitious reverence, and by the influence which concentrated and corporate wealth always acquires, wields power over civil affairs; such an ecclesiastic organism is a menace to the civil power, and becomes dangerous to the liberty of the people and to the peace and good order of society."

Is this an assault upon Mormonism alone? There is not a church, from the great Catholic organization down through all the weakling ecclesiastical products of this religiously weakling age, that is not assaulted by this observation. Take the thought home, Christians! The rest lie easy because it is not brought to their immediate doors ; but the ever-widening circles caused by this pebble in the ocean of religious life will yet drive wickedly against other doors. Just as sure as heaven is the portion of the good, just so sure will a wrong done the Mormon Church, because it violates principle, bring to the doors of other organizations a brood of disasters that cannot be stayed. When Mr. Reed says the keynote of the Mormon problem is that the Mormons, as a church, have a polity, he assaults every organized religion—for all have polities. If Mr. Tucker, as a Christian, can determine legisla-tively what Christianity is, will there not come a time when he, or some other individual inflicted with the religious doc-trines peculiar to his own sect, may rule out of court those not of his mind, as being unchristian, and on this basis justify an assault on their church? In such a rational event could not Mr. Reed, or some believer in his sophistry, say of such an act: "It is useless to call this an assault upon a religion ?" Evil will run its course. We cannot place our hands upon the act done and bring it back. It goes on, so far as we are able to prevent it, for all time. If religious bigotry and sectarian prejudice are dead, then there is no danger. But they are not dead. There is danger. Thus Mormons, in fighting against wrongs heaped upon them in answer to wild and thoughtless demands, are, in their own behalf, actually defending prin-ciples for all mankind, and in behalf of those who have wrought them harm—saving others from themselves. Thus becomes true the assumption that at first blush appeared so arrogantly presumptuous.

The fact that the legislation sought to be imposed upon the people of Utah (and which was, in a modified form, imposed) was not for the suppression of polygamy, is

undeniable.   From the days when ex-Governor Murray
arraigned the Mormon Church in the *North American
Review*, until the latest edition of the organ that defends the
Loyal League, it has been conceded that polygamy was "but
a very small part of the whole business." The Mormons,
because of their numbers, have held political control in the
Territory.   They have been simple enough to hold, in a
degree, the Apostle Paul's behest to the Romans, "Be of the
same mind one toward another." The fruits of unity have
been satisfactory. The minority has not had control of offices.
Hence the trouble.   The disincorporation of the Church
would not alter the political conditions in Utah.   Therefore,
it is determined to invent a test oath to be applied to every
Mormon. This is done. Yet Mormons may take the oath; but
to cover any possible defect, the appointment of every officer
in the Territory, about 3,500 in number, is placed by Mr.
Tucker's bill (which is published at the end of this pamphlet)
in the hands of the Governor, save 108 whom the President is
given the power to appoint, and save members of the House
branch of the Legislature.   These are balanced by thirteen
appointees in the Council branch and then blocked by this
Governor with absolute veto power.   No one can prove such
a move is designed to suppress polygamy. Polygamy was the
cry on which the promoters of this bill hoped to ride into
office and spoils by taxing the Mormon people who then
would have no redress.   But the Territorial Marshal is given
power to arrest any person whom he may think an offender.
This Marshal is appointed by the President, and has authority
to appoint deputies without number, all possessed of the
same powers the bill confers on him.   Was this to suppress
polygamy? when citizens of Utah were even then arrested on
sight and 97 per cent of the persons arrested were convicted?
Then the Utah Commission, charged with the control of
elections in Utah, is retained in position when all elective
officers, save 26 are made appointive, and these 26—members
of the House branch of the Legislature and the Delegate to
Congress—are elected but once in two years.   Was this to
suppress polygamy, or to steal a territory for a minority?
   This minority organized what is called the Loyal League,

in Utah—a secret organization whose members are pledged to secure rule of the Territory by the minority. Each member pays fifty cents a month into the society, the funds to be used for the securing of the end in view by the speediest methods possible. As the representative of this League, R. N. Baskin (who said in a speech before the Judiciary Committee when the Senate bill was being considered and before Mr. Tucker's substitute was reported, that the object was to destroy a "theocracy)" went to Washington. C. W. Bennett went as another lawyer. The League also employed lobbyists; and later on, its prominent members are understood to have joined in a petition to the Governor of Utah, Caleb W. West, asking him to go to Washington and aid in securing the passage of this bill. Whether the rumor be true or not, he did go and did use his influence to have passed a bill which, by the number of appointments it gave him would, had it become law, have made him uncrowned King of the Territory. When the bill had passed the House he received a dispatch from prominent members of the Loyal League which read: "Well done, good and faithful servant?" Was this to suppress polygamy, or to get control of a territory in the interest of the few at the expense of the many? The Utah Commission twice reported that the Edmunds law of 1882 was accomplishing all that could be expected of it and might be relied upon in time to hasten the final extinction of "Mormonism"—not polygamy. Yet the Commission recommended the passage of this bill or a measure embodying its main features. It could not have been the desire to have the bill passed to suppress polygamy, for that, as a part of Mormonism, under the operation of the Edmunds law of March 22, 1882, was already hastening to "extinction." But this Commission recommended that the Governor be given the appointing power "by and with the consent of the Commission." They wanted pap too. They wanted more. Unless some duty of this nature were imposed upon them their occupation was gone. Some excuse must be had for drawing a salary and it might thus be had. What does all this tell? As plain as the writing on the wall, this: Those not now possessed of office, yearned for it. The Governor pined for henchmen, and the Commission hankered for yet more authority, and to have the Governor, in a degree, dependent upon their caprice. It was the greed for place and thirst for power. The people of Utah, with polygamy as a stigma upon them, would long be serfs; and their cries, coming from "vile Mormons only," would be unheeded in this great and free nation. We can now see why "the pending bill," in Mr. Taylor's language, "contemplated more than the suppression of polygamy;" and why Mr. Tucker considered polygamy "only an incident," a "very small part of the whole business;" and, lastly, why Mr. Risden T. Bennett, of North Carolina, unchallenged, designated it as a "job." Read the review of the speeches that follows, and if the whole scope and purpose does not unfold itself into an extended scheme for the destruction of a religious community and their robbery under the protection of law, then indeed there is nothing in the words of men; then the hawk has no design on the barn yard fowl; then the Millennium is come, and the lion and lamb may rest peacefully side by side.

Following comes a review of the speeches made in the House, January 12th, 1887, in behalf of the bill reported to the House by the Judiciary Committee through its chairman, J. Randolph Tucker, as a substitute for the Senate bill. This review has been undertaken for two reasons :

First—Because the speeches embrace nearly, if not all, the salient points ever made against the Mormons; though these, as they appear in different places, assume many strange and fastastic garbs. If it can be shown that the statements are fundamentally contradictary, the whole falls, and there is then left no case against the Mormons. Therefore, they stand acquitted. They have but to show the vain, untrustworthy and inherently destructive statements of their assailants to make a case for themselves.

Second—Because the young are appealed to ever as the hope of redeeming this country from "Mormon dominion." By glib sophistries, by loud acclamations from designing spoilers—traitors to humanity no less than to the nation—it is sought to allure the young from the ways of their fathers and to make eternally blind those already so biased that they can see nothing but treason in Mormons and in their faith. We are told that the future is best to be judged by the past. Let the Mormon youth, let the thoughtful reader, ask and think what the future promises a Mormon in the esteem of these "loyal men," when that future is read and foreshadowed by the light of the past. Half a century ago persecutions began against Mormons. On the summit of these years stand the people against whom this measure was directed. The youthful Mormon and the student may easily trace the road traveled. Along the line of march the earth has been beautified; it has smiled gladly wherever touched by them. In fifteen years the Mormons were driven three times from homes they had made, cities they had built, lands their efforts had blessed. Each time despoiled of all earthly possessions, and still, by the blessing that ever follows industry, they were wealtheir in worldly goods before each successive spoilation and exodus than at the one preceding. Across western wilds the favors of God and of nature, which ever crown the exertions of thrift and virtuous habits, still kept pace with that people. Thousands who abuse, misrepresent, malign and curse them, to-day luxuriate in the results of their self-denial and thrift, and bask in the fruits of a faith, without which eye had never seen the marvels they have wrought. But along this pathway there are also unmistakable traces of relentless persecution—of weary and worn mothers, starving babes at their breasts, the blood of fathers, brothers and husbands. The cry of treason swells in the rising wind, to be lost only with the bitter sobs of the wife and mother among lone graves on trackless prairies and amid the undiscovered depths of majestic mountain chains. But the spirit of persecution never dies. When the object of its hate is again discovered the cry is renewed, gaining volume with each day, and now, on the summit of these years, the wild winds of public clamor again howl treason. The unholy thirst for treasure grows apace. Prejudice and hatred, increasing in intensity with the growth of wicked desires, is yearly, daily, hourly crystallizing against a people, whose faith, despised, ridiculed and condemned though it may be, has nevertheless worked a success admirable in the eyes of the wise and marvelous in the opinion of the students of vexed problems in modern times. Charges, undreamed of once, are now made boldly and believed by much of the American heart because of false alarms, and the treacherous beacon-light of political wreckers. Year by year laws are passed more stringent each than its predecessor, that would not have been dreamed of at first; and these laws, while they may receive the approbation of the unreasoning, must nevertheless be profoundly condemned by those of sober thought and honesty. So gradual these encroachments, they have awakened neither suspicion nor alarm, till to-day, the barrier which should stand between Mormons and slavery, is laid low in the dust, and men do not see it or will not. This from the summit of fifty years. And what for the future? If history, as interpreted by worldly wisdom, teaches ought, may not the youth of Utah read in the unrequited past the story of the future of his people, and with their political death, behold the extinction of human liberty and the disruption of this nation as the crown of civilized governments, the glory of republican principles?

Were it not for the abiding faith which, as the Latter-day Saint religion teaches its members, should be had in the eternal duration of the principles upon which this country is founded, what would the future hold out to young Mormons? If we read the future by the past, there is for the coming Mormons—the youth now asked to throw off as shackles the wise and loving restraints that a father throws about his child to shield him from harm—nothing but wrong at the hands of political tricksters, deprivation under the lash of spoilers and death from the hatred of blinded sectarians. But there is a light in prophecy which penetrates the dim and misty veil of the future. Guided by faith, warmed by the consciousness that eternal truth and never dying justice must prevail, the Mormon youth will still hope on, and the promises of God (that this government, the foundation of which was inspired of Him, shall survive the assaults of traitors under the name of "loyalists" and "liberals" and will again be reverenced by men as of old) will buoy them up in the hour of darkness, enable them to elude the tempter's wiles, and teach them to preserve liberty for themselves by defending it for all the children of

men. I only ask the youth of Zion, and fair minded of the
nation, to read the following pages, and if it is not made
apparent that this generation has inherited and reaped a
harvest of falsehood regarding the Mormon people, then
indeed is their's a hopeless case. If the clamor and rage
against the Mormon people have no better foundation than this
(and it has not) then is the house in which their enemies take
refuge, built on sand; and when the rain of justice descends,
when the wind of righteous public opinion sets in, and the
flood of human kindness shall come and beat against it, that
building will fall, "and great will be the fall of it." It will crush
to eternal shame and contempt all who have taken refuge
within its walls—save only those whom a kindly oblivion shall
already have buried in unfathomable silence.

CHAPTER II.

SPEECH OF HON. E. B. TAYLOR, OF OHIO.—A NEW VERSION OF
   EARLY "MORMON" HISTORY.—ENLIGHTENMENT NEEDED
   ON "CHIEFLY" AND "WHOLLY."—A SOUL-CRUSHING TYR-
   ANNY WITH A REFLECTION ON UNPROMISING RESULTS —
   A NEW DISCOVERY IN MARRIAGE POSSIBILITIES.—A VERSE
   ON CRIMES AGAINST CHASTITY, WITH A TAIL PIECE ON
   CHURCH AND STATE, AND AN APPENDIX ON OBTAINING
   UNOBTAINABLE INFORMATION. — WANTED — A CASE OF
   STRANGULATION.—THE "JOB" DISCLOSED.

MR. EZRA B. TAYLOR. Mr. Speaker, the pending
   measure contemplates more than the suppression of
   polygamy, and invites inquiry as to its scope and a
brief history of the circumstances which have resulted in the
necessity for legislative action.

COMMENT. This quotation is made for later use, when it
will be seen that you urge the bill on the main ground of
polygamy.

TAYLOR. Joseph Smith was killed in an Illinois jail in 1844, after which those who had followed him, some 20,000 in number, emigrated to the far west, and settled around Salt Lake in 1847, in a region of country belonging to Mexico.

COMMENT. The Mormons did not "emigrate." This fact is notorious. They were brutally driven from their homes. It requires little sense to detect the difference in the meaning of the words. Mr. Taylor being a Congressman, a legislator, the presumption is only fair that he chose the words carefully to mislead.

TAYLOR. When the Territorial government [of Utah] went into operation, Brigham Young, having been appointed governor by the President, the conduct of affairs continued as before—wholly in the hands of the Mormons, and chiefly in the hands of the Church.

COMMENT. That the conduct of affairs should continue in the hands of Mormons is not surprising for several palpable reasons: In whose hands, if not of Mormons, could they continue, since only Mormons were there? So far as Mormons, being the only persons there, were in official positions, so far only was the Church interested. If the offices were "wholly in the hands of the Mormons," and Mormons alone were there, and they, as you assert later on, are bound to the Church by the most tyrannical ties, how can it be that the concerns of the state were only "chiefly in the hands of the Church." Why this loop hole between "wholly" and "chiefly?" Is it a stagger at truth with a deflection in the direction of falsehood? But "wholly" or "chiefly" as you will, what evil was there in state affairs continuing in the hands of the Mormons? What evil now? Mormons were, and Mormons are in the majority; they had and still have by far the greater interests at stake in securing a good government. What kind of a country did you or do you want? Mormons, being there alone, held the offices. That was republicanism. What on earth did you want them to do, since this is an evil?

TAYLOR. The Territorial Legislature declared valid the acts incorporating the Church and the Emigration Fund Company, *and those incorporations have since been the sources of power and the agents of the all-crushing* tyranny exerted in Utah.

COMMENT. The italicised words are untrue. This charge has again and again been made without a scintilla of proof. The time for unchallenged assertion has passed. But do you hold that a soul-crushing tyranny which takes the poor of this and of other lands, gives to them homes, lifts them in the scale of humanity, as these agencies have done? The last census shows that 90 per cent of Mormon heads of families own their homes. Would not a little of such soul-crushing tyranny be a Godsend to other parts even of this enlightened nation?

TAYLOR. Congress in 1862 passed a law punishing bigamy and polygamy, but no considerable result followed the enactment, and in 1882 the Edmunds law, so called, was passed, and has been somewhat more productive of convictions, but does not promise success in its object, because of the difficulties of making proof.

COMMENT. All reliable evidence contradicts this declaration. This matter was up before the House Judicary Committee which reported the bill you advocate, and the evidence there gives you a flat contradiction. You were a member of that committee. Cases where the law fails, as interpreted and executed, are the rarest exceptions. The report of the Governor of Utah, Caleb W. West, made some time prior to the delivery of your speech, showed the mumber of convictions that have been secured under the brutal operation of the law which you assert "does not promise success in its object?" That report shows that but three per cent of the persons arrested have failed of conviction. Where will Mr. Taylor find a parallel to this? In cases of polygamy and unlawful cohabitation arrest and conviction have become interchangeable terms. Even the Utah Commission, which advocated the passage of this, or a measure embodying its main features, reported that the execution of the law of 1882 was having a perceptible effect, and in time might be fairly relied upon to break up the practice against which it was aimed. Put the statements of these parties (the Governor of Utah and the Utah Commission) against those of this legislator, compare all with the facts and what shall we name the conclusion? What shall we say of this legislator? Still another point:

"The difficulties of making proof." It is a fact that but three per cent of those arrested escape conviction. Therefore you either state falsely when you say the law "does not promise success in its object," because of "the difficulties of making proof," or Mormons are convicted and punished without proof. If you state truly, then the men in Utah charged with the execution of the law are vindictive scoundrels. You cannot escape this conclusion, and I shall not dispute it, though clearly you did not mean it; ninety-seven per cent of convictions prove it. What human purpose could prompt a sane man to such flagrant violations of truth? Every conviction of a Mormon for polygamy or unlawful cohabitation has been almost entirely on Mormon testimony; and in numberless cases the evidence was furnished by the accused himself, who preferred the full penalty of the law to making a defense when that defense would subject his family, wives and children, to the most indecent and brutal interrogations. That the testimony warranted the convictions had is a different matter. Good lawyers say no. The Supreme Court of the United States has sustained that opinion in cases.

TAYLOR. In Utah there are no records of marriages, either of the first or of the succeeding ones. None but officers of the Church can solemnize marriage, and those marriages succeeding the first only take place under circumstances of the greatest secrecy.

COMMENT. The testimony before your committee on this subject was that in Utah any person could perform the marriage ceremony. This was the testimony of Hon. F. S. Richards, a lawyer and a Mormon. No attempt has been made to deny it. The fact is irrefutable, and yet we are told that "none but Church officers can solemnize marriages." Had you stated that, according to Mormon doctrines, all Mormons were required to be married by Church officers you had told a truth. But you did not say that. In proof: Every denominational minister performs marriages; the Justices of the United States Courts solemnize marriages; the Justices of the Peace do marry applicants. There then being no marriage law the parties could marry themselves in Utah. They have done so, making it a civil contract.

TAYLOR. Under the Territorial government there *have been no* laws punishing crimes against chastity, such as incest, bigamy, or even adultery, excepting the last, against which provision was made only in case the husband or wife of the guilty party prosecuted.

COMMENT. If you think as loosely as you write or speak, the proper place for you is not in Congress but an asylum. There have been Territorial laws against crimes of unchastity. This fact should be known by a man who says he spoke "after long and earnest study of the subject." What you meant to say, or should have said, is: There *are* "no laws punishing crimes against chastity," etc. But Mr. Taylor has already said that the "conduct of affairs continued as before— wholly in the hands of Mormons," and that the Church and Emigration Fund Company have been "the sources of power and the agents of the all-crushing tyranny exerted in Utah;" and he will declare later that the Church is "not an empire in an empire, but the empire itself." If this be true, then the Church dominates the state; its laws become the laws of the state. Now it is a fact that the most stringent laws of the Church are against unchastity—coming under which head are crimes, and the only crimes, that cannot be forgiven. Out of this fact has grown the wild charge, which has doubtless reached your ears, that the Mormons not only believe in, but also advocate and practice blood atonement. We will hear you say in a few minutes: The "Church governs all things with a steady hand; it disposes of life and liberty, it dictates laws." In view of these assertions what becomes of your point that there have been no laws against unchastity? If, as you say, the "Church absorbs as well as controls the state," then you forge an untruth when you say there are no laws against unchastity. If there are no laws against unchastity, then you forge an untruth when you say the "Church absorbs as well as controls the state." Take the dilemma at either end, you will find it too hot to hold.

TAYLOR. It [polygamy] is now growing stronger, and is not confined to the boundaries of Utah.

COMMENT. I defy you to prove this assertion. What

testimony there is on the subject proves the reverse of what
you state. The Utah Commission, in a report to the Secretary of the Interior, for 1884, writes thus of the anti-polygamy
law of March 22, 1882:

We have more than once in our former reports suggested that as the
Government has to deal here with a people who are wonderfully superstitious and fanatically devoted to their system of religion, the public
should not expect, as the immediate result of the present laws of Congress, nor indeed of any legislation, however radical, the sudden over-
throw of polygamy, and we now repeat, the most that can be predicted of
such legislation is that it will, if no step backward is taken, soon ameliorate the harder conditions of Mormonism and hasten the day for its final
extinction.

In its last report the Commission uses this language:

Whether, upon the whole, polygamous marriages are on the decrease
in Utah is a matter on which different opinions are expressed, but undoubtedly many persons have been restrained by the fear of disfranchisement and the penitentiary, and we think it is safe to say that in the more
enlightened portion of the Territory, as for example Salt Lake City and
its vicinity, very few polygamous marriages have occurred within the last
year, while, on the other hand, in some parts of the Territory they have
reason to believe that it is otherwise.

This is the most reliable testimony available. It comes from
a source that is constantly protesting its anxiety to secure the
extinction of Mormonism, and I suppose no one will question
the sincerity of its protestations. But Mr. Taylor has said
the Edmunds anti-polygamy law of 1882 does not promise
success in its object. In the teeth of this assertion we not
only have ninty-seven per cent. of convictions, but two reports
from the authorized agents of the government, the open oppo-
nents of Mormonism, in the first of which we are told this
law will

"Soon ameliorate the harder conditions of Mormonism and hasten
the day for its final extinction,"

And in the second that

"Undoubtedly many persons have been restrained [from polygamous
practices] by the fear of disfranchisement and the penitentiary, * * *
In the more enlightened portion of the Territory, * * * very
few polygamous marriages have occurred within the last year," [1886].

Do you give your information as more reliable than this? Where did you get it? These facts were before the House when it voted for the bill you are advocating; were before it when you voted for it.

But a pertinent question is: How did you get your information or the Utah Commission theirs? You have said the law of 1882 "does not promise success in its object." Is it not a fair interpretation to say this means there were very few convictions? You have also said that polygamous marriages

"Only take place under circumstances of the greatest secrecy."

How then do you know that polygamy is growing stronger? How then is it that when arrests are of daily and nightly occurrence, but three per cent. of those arrested escape? Does not this again suggest that the testimony on which they are convicted is insufficient, or that you have again made a characteristically reckless declaration? As the law is vigorously enforced, there must be convictions where there is guilt—the conviction of the ninty-seven per cent. of persons arrested shows this. But if this law does not promise success, it must be because it fails of securing convictions, which is not the case; or is it a failure because the convictions are not sufficiently numerous? If that be so, then the vigorous enforcement of the law, coupled with the insufficiency of convictions, proves that the law does promise success in its results; for the absence of convictions viewed in connection with the number of convictions to the arrests, proves that offenses under the law are rare.

But if these marriages only take place under circumstances of the greatest secrecy, how comes it that you know polygamy is on the increase? How comes it there is so great a percentage of convictions to the number of arrests? And how do you learn that this growth is "not confined to boundaries of Utah?" And why, in view of this fact—admitting it to be such—do you legislate only for Utah? I defy human ingenuity to devise a method by which any being can more successfully "mix himself up" than you have succeeded in doing. And this is an American legislator!

3

TAYLOR. Its friends, the Legislature of Utah, will not strangle it, [polygamy] but Congress must, and fortunately Congress can. It has the legal power under the Constitution, and it has the means at hand.

COMMENT. Greater men than you deny that Congress has the Constitutional power. Heaven knows if it depended upon your utterances, its constitutionality might be questioned by every bootblack and scavenger in the land. But admitting you are right, will you kindly explain in what way this bill attempts to stop the practice. I say its last and least purpose is the suppression of polygamy. Since assertion is the rule, I say its purpose from inception to conclusion is the robbery and enslaving of a people. Do you forget that you opened your remarks by saying "the pending bill contemplates more than the suppression of polygamy?" What else is there connected with the Mormon people that is criminal or that you dare make punishable either by fine or imprisonment? What is this more that is contemplated? Silent! Yes silent, and for once wise! Other members of the committee which reported the bill—the committee itself—the bill's chief outside advocate—declared the purpose to be the destruction of a theocracy. Mr. Bennett, of North Carolina, in his speech declared "it was a job." The bill itself, in every line and feature, says it was a "job"—a determination to rob and enslave the Mormon people. This is the other end contemplated.

CHAPTER III.

TAYLOR'S SPEECH CONTINUED.—FANATICISM DEFINED AND A
REMINDER SUGGESTED.—MR. TAYLOR DISCOVERS A NEW
METHOD OF SEIZURE.—ANOTHER REMINDER WITH A DIS-
SERTATION ON HOW TO SEIZE, AND WHEN IT CANNOT BE
DONE.—A STARTLING MILITARY SEIZURE OF THE SAME
ORDER.—MR. TAYLOR'S EMPIRE, THE ONLY ONE ON
EARTH.—A CAPITAL CASE AGAINST A CHURCH, AND IT
WILL NOT HOLD WATER. — FREEDOM OF WORSHIP. — TO
STOP CRIME.—AN UNALTERABLE OPPOSITION WHICH IS
NOT UNALTERABLE.

TAYLOR. An earnest, resolute, and even fanatical people have taken possession of one of the large Territories of the Union.

COMMENT. This is as clear as mud. Who says the people are fanatical? Mr. Taylor. All hail! There can be no more dispute as to what is fanatical. It is painful but necessary constantly to remind you of what you have previously asserted. You have already used these words:

"Joseph Smith was killed in an Illinois jail in 1844, after which those who had followed him, some 20,000 in number, emigrated to the far west, *and settled around Salt Lake in 1847, a region of country belonging to Mexico.*"

COMMENT. The italics are mine. Now you say this "fanatical people *have taken possession of one of the large Terri- tories of the Union."* On your own word they went to the country they now occupy when it belonged to Mexico. What it is to-day, the joy of those who admire the fruits of honest and persevering toil, and the cause of an uneasy itch on the part of those who would steal it, and rob and enslave its people, what there is to it, is there because the Mormons have made it. This is how the Mormons have taken posses- sion of one of the large Territories of the Union. How cowardly, how contemptible the part of one who would detract from the unfriendly, rob the most vile even of the deserved mead of praise. In the heat of debate extravagant utterances are sometimes pardonable, but that a legislator of the greatest nation on earth should be guilty of such cowardly imbecility, in deliberate black and white! 'Tis enough to make the nether angels weep!

TAYLOR. They [the fanatical people] seized upon the public domain.

COMMENT. But it was the domain of Mexico. You have said so. Why do you complain? Even were it not so, has not all this land been paid for? Why then say "seized?" If you have no better conception of the value of words, the kindergarten and not Congress is the place for you.

TAYLOR. [A fanatical people] established a Church which absorbs as well as controls the state.

COMMENT. What about the absence of laws against crimes of unchastity then? The Church and the state are one, if the latter is absorbed. Therefore, if the Church have laws against unchastity, the state, being one with the Church, also has laws against these sins and crimes. Why then did you say that "under the Territorial government there have been no laws punishing crimes against chastity," etc.

TAYLOR. [A fanatical people] seized all the civil power, including the education of children.

COMMENT. Again we have the word "seized." There could have been neither civil nor ecclesiastical power in Utah, as there would have been occasion for none, until it was inhabited by men. Those who first locate in a place, be it where it may, are the source of human power there. Power could not be seized of men till men were clothed with power, and the Mormons, coming here and finding no human power, could seize none. Hence, they did not "seize" power, neither civil nor ecclesiastical. Such as they had they brought with them. By their efforts in habiting and building up this part of the country, which subsequently became part of the United States domain, they made it possible for a republican government to establish its agents in this section. It did so. The power the Mormons hold to-day, the power they have held since this land fell to the United States, and a Territorial form of government was established here—save always that which is above all governments, which comes from the Eternal One alone—is the gift of the United States; and being a gift it could not be seized by those to whom it was given. Perhaps you will understand now that you sometimes use words as the amateur violinist does the fiddle—without skill and to the disgust of all who hear you.

The Church, as such, does not attempt to interfere with the education of children. Schools, operated under Territorial law, are free from religious instructions. This fact is so widely known, has been so widely published, that one cannot believe you ignorant of it. Draw your own conclusion from this remark.

TAYLOR. [A fanatical people] seized the whole military force and gave it into the hands of the Church.

COMMENT. But there was no military force in Utah when the Mormons first reached that land. How then could they seize it? You have also said the territory was originally "wholly" Mormon, and the offices were "chiefly" in their hands. How could they "seize" that which they already possessed, which could belong to no one but themselves? Except the United States army, there has been no military force in Utah for over fifteen years; the militia was disbanded by Governor Schafer, in 1870? Do you mean to say the United States army in Utah has been seized by the Mormons and given into the hands of the Church? If not, what do you mean? Does it not begin to dawn on you that you have been talking insufferable rubbish?

TAYLOR. [The Church] is not an empire in an empire, but *the* empire itself.

COMMENT. Hear him, ye gods! This "empire itself," the Church,or the Territory of Utah, as you like,sends a Delegate to each Congress of the United States; it has accepted from the the United States a Territorial form of government; upon this "empire" are imposed, by the United States, a governor with absolute veto power, a commission which directs all elections, a secretary, judges, prosecuting attorneys, marshals, surveyors, persons through whom only the land of the "empire" can be had by giving money to the United States, revenue collectors, postmasters, and for this "empire" laws are framed by Congress, under the operation of which the most noted men in the Territory, the kings of this "empire," and its potentates, flee in dread of laws which are repugnant to the "empire" and to its leaders; to the United States Territorial courts in this "empire itself," cases are constantly being taken; the subjects of "this empire" hold themselves amenable to United States courts and officers, and they appeal from United States courts to United States courts until that of last resort has been reached; the people of this "empire itself" believe, and so proclaim, the Constitution of the United States to have been inspired of God. And this "is not an empire in an empire, but *the* empire itself." What language could adequately describe the insufferableness of this twaddle?

TAYLOR. That Church governs all things with a steady and relentless hand, it disposes of life and liberty; it dictates laws and practices, and has, in the name of religion, imposed upon its subjects faith in and practice of polygamy.

COMMENT. To all these statements (in the spirit I comprehend them to be given by you), I give the most unqualified lie. If it governed all things with a steady and relentless hand, death would be the portion of those who apostatized; who by trying to undermine it would be traitors to the church. I adopt herein your conclusion, for you charge that it "disposes of life and liberty." That is a wilful and malicious lie. The proof? It is seen in the protection afforded every rank apostate who hates and labors to destroy the Church, yet who thrives and prospers; the proof is in the person of every man who raises his voice against the religion and the people, who nevertheless lives here and grows wealthy apace; it is found in the men who give of their means to secure legislation that will place the people of Utah at their mercy. The proof is in the conduct of United States judges and prosecuting attorneys who distort the laws and send Mormons to prison, and who turn loose upon the community licentious and degraded scoundrels; it is seen in the killing of Mormons by Gentiles and apostates clothed with the majesty of United States authority, and who are acquitted and returned to honor; it is seen in the fleeing of Mormons honored and esteemed; it is seen in the business depression of the Territory! Turn where you will, whether to social, ecclesiastical, business or material quarters and there, as indelible as the wrongs that have been heaped for years upon the Mormon people, is written, deep and damning proof—till there is nothing but proof. It is a falsehood, a base, unqualified, unmitigated falsehood.

The Church does not impose upon its subjects the practice of polygamy. The testimony before your committee by a Mormon, Mr. Richards, was that it was permissive. The United States Congress ousted Hon. Geo. Q. Cannon from his seat in that body, not because he was a Mormon, but because he was a polygamist. This was notice that no professing polygamist should again sit in Congress. Hon. John T. Caine, who represents Utah as delegate, a member for several years with you, is a Mormon and was. You knew him to be one. You knew he could not sit there as a member were he a polygamist; and yet you had the hardihood to say that the Mormon Church imposed upon its subjects the practice of polygamy? Can you help being contemptible in your own eyes?

TAYLOR. This bill undertakes *   *   * to insure in Utah, as elsewhere, equality of rights to all churches, giving all freedom of worship and of conscience, but also subjecting all to the laws of the land.

COMMENT. The presence in Utah of denominational churches, with ministers who make a practice not only of denouncing Mormons and their faith on the platform and in the pulpit in Utah, but who make periodical visits east and west, and by abundant abuse of this people and their faith, gather in the needful dollar, show that freedom of worship is one of the most unquestioned facts regarding Utah. Correlative proof is established by the presence of large schools operated in the interest of religions opposed to Mormon belief, and which have been founded with the avowed purpose of winning from the Mormon faith the offspring of Mormon parents. And it is the boast of these institutions that they are making good headway.

But this bill is not designed to insure freedom of worship. That were needless. Its purpose is to reach and search the conscience of every Mormon, and while it may fail in its ulterior purpose—the immediate slavery of the Mormon people—it has nevertheless been successful in touching the consciences of many who only believe certain things, but who have broken no law and who design to break none. Its design was to rob Mormons of the manliness of citizenship. You know that was its purpose; you knew it when you said it was intended to secure freedom of worship.

TAYLOR. This bill proposes * * * to place the government of Utah largely in the hands of officers appointed by the President of the United States, *not only that crime may cease, but that good government may exist.*

COMMENT. What reason was there for this proposed course? What authority have you for stating that good government does not exist in Utah, and has not existed? and if good government does exist what becomes of your talk about evils existing? Before your committee, treating on this subject, Hon. Jeff. Chandler made the appended statement. It was never challenged. It was never denied. The reason was that challenge and denial were impossible:

The Gentiles come here with a representative [R. N. Baskin] who tells you that he has lived in that Territory for twenty years, and during that time this so-called Mormon element held absolute political power within the Territory of Utah. They made all the laws that affect the domestic welfare of all the people living in that Territory, and yet, during the three hours which he occupied in his argument before this committee he could not, or did not, recollect a single instance where the Gentile population, though in a small minority, have been unequally or unjustly treated by this legislation. Now, so far as they present themselves here as a class they state no grievance against themselves. They do not come here and say that the political power of Utah ought to be taken out of the hands of this majority because the majority uses that power oppressively against them. Not at all. They do not say that taxation is unequal or unjust or that any privileges are denied them which are enjoyed by the majority, or that there is anything in the domestic government which gives them the slightest cause to complain. Do they say that they receive unfair treatment in the courts of Utah? Not at all. Do they show you a single instance in the adjudication of that Territory from its creation down to this hour wherein the Gentiles have not been fairly and justly treated by the courts? Not at all. Then what do they complain of? It is that the majority does not deport itself in a manner to excite the approval of the minority. A population of 150,000 does not in all things conduct itself so as to meet the absolute and unqualified approval of 30,000, and therefore they ask that the political power of the majority shall be taken away from these 150,000 and left with the minority.

TAYLOR. All these objects meet my most unqualified approbation after long and earnest study of the subject. I am, therefore, pained to find one provision in the bill to which I am *unalterably opposed.* For a long time female suffrage has prevailed in Utah, as in other Territories, with no known evils connected with it. This bill strikes that down without any complaint as to the manner in which it has been exercised and without any allegation of danger in the future exercise. * * * Will the precedent be invoked hereafter, and if so, in what direction? Who can tell? In spite of this objection, I shall earnestly support the bill.

COMMENT. But notwithstanding an *unalterable* opposition, an appalling suggestion, and a couple of queries, you alter your opposition, and in the next breath promise earnestly to support that to which you declare yourself unalterably opposed. Human endurance is exhausted. It is but justice to the race to assume this to be the only example of the kind on record. Let us pray so.

It is most improbable that a knave could be half so stupid or contradictory. There is scarcely a statement in your speech that, in its terms or spirit, might not be successfully controverted. I could almost challenge any being, the most astute and ingenuous, to bring, within smaller compass, more contradictory assertion. Wnat you do say is not significant; it is not original; but it does possess, nevertheless, one clear and distinguishing characteristic: It is villianously untrue, and you have furnished the proof yourself.

CHAPTER IV.

HON. T. B. REED'S SPEECH.—AN ADORER OF LOCAL SELF GOV-
ERNMENT.—THE DISTRICT OF COLUMBIA AND THE TERRI-
TORIES. — A LINE ABOUT FEE SIMPLE. — RIGHTS THAT
ARE PRIVILEGES AND PRIVILEGES THAT ARE RIGHTS.—A
SORRY DILEMMA.—JUDGE BLACK TO THE RESCUE.—THE
MORMONS LEAVE WITHOUT LEAVING. — HOW MORMONS
TAKE FROM THE UNITED STATES WHAT BELONGS TO
MEXICO.—A SHAKEN REED.

BUT if Mr. Taylor is a featherweight, the same cannot be
said of Mr. T. B. Reed, of Maine, to whose remarks the
following criticisms seem just. It may be stated that Mr. Reed
began his twenty minutes' speech by protesting his unqualified
approval of local self government. "I am a believer in local
self-government. I am also a thorough believer in government by the people, and I look upon many of the tendencies
—temporary I trust—of modern times with great distrust; for
instance, the tendency *to take from the people of this country
their power of frequent examination into the acts of their
officials.*"

REED. Gentlemen who have discussed this question upon
the other side have done so always under the implied
assumption that the Territory of the United States occupies
the same relation to the United States as the Territory of a
State.

COMMENT. This is not a fact. They argued simply on the
assumption that a man who, in a State, was a citizen of the
United States, continued to be one even when he went into
a Territory. This fact is not denied in theory. In practice,
however, so far as Utah is concerned, a citizen loses many of
his rights, and the bill then under discussion proposed to
establish the condition of complete servitude beyond equivo-
cation.

REED. The right of self-government is a right which
exists in a State, which belongs to the inhabitants of the

State, and which the Constitution declares Congress shall guarantee to the State. But the territory owned by the United States occupies an entirely different relation. Why, here in this district, before our very eyes, has been established, amid the acclamations of gentlemen on the other side, a government which does not allow the residents of a city of 200,000 inhabitants the least power or control over the affairs of the land they inhabit. It allows them neither control over their own local affairs nor participation, as citizens of the United States, in the common affairs of the country. This arises from the peculiar situation of the territory which is occupied by the seat of Government.

COMMENT. The point you endeavor to make here, as it rests on a fallacious assumption, is valueless. In the first place the Constitution distinctly provides for such territory as the District of Columbia, and gives Congress exclusive jurisdiction over that section only. It does not provide for what is now a Territory. Such a government was never contemplated by the framers of the Constitution. This fact is undeniable. In the second place, the rule prevailing in the District of Columbia is applied to the Territories only by a strained and arbitrary reading—so strained and so at variance with the republican spirit of the Constitution, that the first republican who advanced the idea, which so many now deem correct, was ashamed of his own claim—though it prevailed. In the course of Hon. Jeff Chandler's argument before the House Judiciary Committee when considering the Edmunds bill as it passed the Senate, and before Mr. Tucker offered his substitute, the following dialogue took place, relating to this point:

MR. CHANDLER. The Territories of the United States have been permitted to govern themselves without exception for the last sixty years. There was an exceptional government established in the Territory of Florida at one time, but only to meet a temporary state of affairs. Since that time the people of the Territories have been allowed to govern themselves.

MR. STEWART. All except you people here in Washington.

MR. CHANDLER. Here the government owns us body and soul. They own our parks and buildings; they own our streets, and we have but little to govern ourselves about.

THE CHAIRMAN. [Mr. Tucker.] Would not the reverse proposition, in some degree, be true—that you own the government?

MR. CHANDLER. Not at all. I think the most insignificant position a man can occupy in Washington is to be a simple citizen. If he is not clothed with power he may not be a man to be looked upon with contempt, but he is regarded with the most painful indifference. But they do not propose to establish such a government in Utah as we have here. Here you have a committee for the District of Columbia alone, and besides you own three-fourths of everything that is worth owning in the District. Then, again, a conference is constantly going on between the agencies you establish for government and yourselves. You do not give the Commissioners any power to legislate, as is asked for in Utah.

But even if the points here taken were not true, it does not follow that the citizens of the District of Columbia are not entitled to the right of suffrage. Is the growing desire for local government within the District opposed to the spirit of the Constitution? Even the fearless Reed dare not claim that. Does the colossal representative from the timber-covered hills and herring shores of Maine hold that he loses any rights as a citizen becase he resides part of the time in the District of Columbia? When he makes these admissions—he will never make them—then his point about the Territories of the United States being as the District of Columbia will have some merit in it; but not until then.

REED. Now, what is the position of a Territory of the United States? It is land owned by the United States outside of the territory of the States themselves. Even when the fee simple has passed, it is our domain.

COMMENT. Granted; but is not this just as true of a State? Certainly. Then if you possess it in a Territory only as you do in a State, your whole point fails, for you have already marked a difference. You dare not apply the doctrine to a State that you do to a Territory. It was simply childish to argue that because the domain, even when the fee simple has passed, belongs to the United States, you can therefore control it and its inhabitants as you choose. If your point rests on this, it is worthless; if it does not rest on this, then difficulty will be experienced in ascertaining what under heaven you mean.

REED. Congress has allowed to the inhabitants of the organized Territories the exercise of certain political privileges. *These have been accorded* to the temporary residents there, *not as rights,but as privileges extended by the hand of Congress.*

COMMENT. Then a citizen of the United States has no *rights*, only *privileges* accorded him? Can it be possible that Mr. Reed will damn his own point? Let us see. A few minutes later, referring to the entrance of the Mormon Pioneers into the valleys of Utah, he uses these words:

REED. They [the Mormons] knew nothing of the value of the mineral lands; and years afterward the swarming miners, when they went there, found themselves, except as to mineral privileges, deprived of *all the rights which fairly belonged to them as citizens of the United States.*

COMMENT. This is painful. You declare in one breath that people in Territories have no *rights*, only *privileges*; then you say they were deprived of *"all rights* which fairly belonged to them as citizens of the United States." Will you please state which time you were correct? Have they rights or have they none? You have advanced [both theories. Reliable as you are, even Mormon faith is unequal to this demand. We will let Judge Black decide, as you are doubtful, or equally positive on two inherently contradictory propositions. You can stand to be pitted against Black, if he can.

JUDGE BLACK. It is true, also, that the general government may give the colonists a charter, and call it an act of incorporation or an organic act. This was what the imperial government of England did for the several colonies that settled on its land in America. But the charter must be a free one. If it abridges the liberty of the people to do as they please about matters which concern nobody else, it is void. Even if the colonists could consent, for a consideration, to accept an organic act imposing restraint upon their right of self-government, they could throw it off as a nullity; for the birthright of a freeman is inalienable. I need not say that foreigners naturalized are on a level with native citizens.

As Congress cannot give, so it cannot withhold the blessing of popular government in a Territory. But the legislation now proposed, in addition to that already passed, would blacken the character of the federal government with an act of cruel perfidy. The charter you gave to Utah was in full

accordance with the broad principle of American liberty.
You organized for them a free territorial government, put into
their hands all the machinery that was needed to carry it on;
the ballot to be used under regulations of their own; officers
chosen by themselves to administer their local affairs, collect
the taxes and take charge of their money, and a legislature
representing them—responsible to them—clothed with exclusive power to make their laws, and to alter them from time to
time as experience might show to be just and expedient.
Gilding your invitation with this offer of free government, you
attracted people from every state and from all parts of the
civilized world, whose industry scattered plenty over that
barren region and made the desert bloom like a garden. Now
you are urged to break treacherously in upon their security;
supersede the laws which they approve by others which are
odious to them; make their legislation a mockery by declar-
ing that yours is exclusive; drive out the officers in whom they
confide, and fill their places with raging and rapacious enemies; take away their right of suffrage, and with it all chance
of peaceable redress; break down the whole structure of the
territorial government, under which you promised to give
them a permanent shelter. Would not this be a case of punic
faith? Apart from all question of constitutional morality, the
conduct of the wrecker who burns false lights to mislead the
vessel he wishes to plunder does not seem to me more perfid-
ious."

REED. A long time ago a body of religionists *left the
United States*, marched across the plains, and *took possession
of certain property belonging to the people of the United States*,
out of which we had determined, in pursuance of our general
policy, to make some day a State.

COMMENT. The italicized words are quoted simply to
show that it is one of your failings, on this subject at least, to
be contradictory. Perhaps you will kindly explain how the
people *left* the United States and still remained *in* the United
States.

The people left the United States because they were three
times driven from homes they had made, from lands they had
paid the United States government for in honest money earned
by honest toil. These lands have never been returned to
them. To this day no Mormon has received a dollar of compensation for his losses; nor the original price of the lands in
the possession of which he was guaranteed by this government. The statesman from Maine would hide the fact that

Mormons were "driven" under the term "left," as his feather-weight compatriot, Taylor, attempted to cover the outrage under the term "emigrated."

But the last quotation from you contains a palpable untruth. The Mormons did not take "possession of certain property belonging to the United States." They left in the United States land that belonged to them. They took possession of "certain property belonging" to Mexico; and on an eminence that overlooks what is now Salt Lake City, these Mormons planted the flag of that country whose President had said, when they appealed to him for protection in their "own land:" "Your cause is just, but I can do nothing for you." Very different from what you charge them with—very different, for this is true. And later on you are compelled to make this admission in answer to a question put to you by Hon. P. A. Collins, of Massachusetts.

CHAPTER V.

REED'S SPEECH CONTINUED.—A CHURCH WITH A POLITY.—WHAT IS A POLITY?—A HINT ON CHURCH USES.—AN APPLICATION IN A NEW QUARTER.—A STATESMAN'S DUTY.—AN UNSOUNDED KEYNOTE.—MR. REED AS AN HISTORIAN.—WOEFUL DISCREPANCIES.—THE NEW HIERARCHY.—RELIGION UNASSAULTED.—A LAWYER IGNORANT OF LAW.—PLEADING IN IGNORANCE.—A RETURN OF LOVE FOR SELF-GOVERNMENT.—SUCH TESTIMONY.—A HOPELESS ASSAULT.

REED. But it was not merely a band of religionists; it was a people that had a polity. The Delegate from Utah himself, either in a moment of forgetfulness when he wrote his manuscript, or in a moment of forgetfulness when he was talking, spoke of "the Mormon polity." There is the keynote of the situation. Those people went out there as the representatives of a polity. They went there as a government.

COMMENT. According to Webster "polity" has two meanings. With the instinct of a lawyer, whose ambition, above truth even, is to succeed, you have adopted the one meaning which alone could give ground to stand upon in the argument that follows: "The form or constitution of a civil government by which a nation or a State is organized. The framework or organization by which the various departments of a civil government are combined into a systematic whole." This is one of Webster's definitions, and on the strength of it, you say of the Mormons: "They went there as a government." There is much cheap talk in this age of church interference in temporal affairs. Perhaps some genius will explain how any church can have excuse for existence if its purpose be not to affect temporal affairs through its members. To say it can have an excuse for existence, and not reach temporal things, is to talk insufferable nonsense. All churches have temporal concerns. Are not all temporal affairs in some manner related to the civil government? Where can the line be drawn? What Congressman dare draw it? Has not every church, therefore, a polity? If that be treason, has Mr. Reed, apart from Mormons, the manhood to say so? Dare he say it of the Catholic or the Methodist church? Mr. Reed dare not. Let us apply Mr. Reed's reason in a new direction, and note its results. The Republican party, of which the Maine Congressman is so distinguished a representative, has a "polity." It could not exist without it. And its polity is purely one referring to civic concerns. As this country is Democratic, should not every Republican, on Mr. Reed's basis, be disfranchised because he belongs to an institution which has a "polity," that polity differing from the polity of the Democracy, which is to-day in the ascendant? Mr. Reed should be ashamed of his argument.

Mr. Webster's second definition of polity (and it follows on the heels of the other, as a part of it, by the use of the word "hence") is: "The form or constitution by which *any institution* is *organized*; the recognized *principles* which lie at the foundation of *any human institution.*" Is the Republican party not an "institution?" A "human institution?" Has it no "organization?" Has it no "principles?" If Mr. Reed can make these admissions then the Republican party has no "polity;" then Mr. Reed's position, while it renders a Mormon unfit for citizenship, may yet leave him loyal, but not otherwise. Mr. Reed dare make no such admissions. Mr. Reed forgot to use his brains. He did a very popular thing.

REED. The Delegate from Utah himself, either in a moment of forgetfulness when he wrote his manuscript, or in a moment of forgetfulness when he was talking, spoke of "the Mormon polity."

COMMENT. The Delegate did not forget himself. The only place in his speech where the word "polity" is used is in a quotation, made from a man, who, like Mr. Reed, is not a Mormon, but who, unlike Mr. Reed, was using his brains to tell the truth, not to indulge in watery sophistry. This gentleman was referring to Mormonism as a church, as an institution within the second definition of the word "polity" which I have given; and if Mr. Reed had been as anxious for information as he was to make a speech against Mormons, he would have listened to the debate instead of writing letters and might thereby have avoided a blunder because of which a man of principle could not rest till righted, and which a reasoner would blush for because of its pettifogging lineaments.

REED. The Delegate from Utah himself, either in a moment of forgetfulness when he wrote his manuscript, or in a moment of forgetfulness when he was talking, and spoke of "the Mormon polity." There is the keynote of the situation.

COMMENT. Well, suppose they had a polity. Is there anything wrong about it? Let us admit they have a civil polity which does not harmonize with yours. If their polity, by its results, after ample time for mature developement, proves to answer the purposes of life better than your polity, what is the duty of a statesman? Unqualifiedly to adopt the better polity. You have not proved the Mormons to have a polity in the sense which you designed should be understood. If they have a polity in any civil sense you have not proved that it is opposed to the one upon which the United States are founded. But if they have a polity, and if it does differ from that of the

United States, you have not proved, nor attempted to prove, that the Mormon polity is not the superior one. "There is the keynote of the situation." You have not touched it. You dare not touch it. Yet with the adroitness of an expert pleader you would lead to the belief that you had sounded the keynote from its lowest note to the topmost.

REED. What did they do? With that rare foresight which indicates statesmanship, and which we should compliment if the object had been just, the Mormon Church took possession, under the forms of law, of every acre of arable land. The land out there required to be irrigated; and they took possession of every source of water supply. They took possession of the forests.

COMMENT. This simply shows how unreliable you are. The bill refers to an entire Territory; the purpose of it, in some respects, to other Territories. Neither the Mormon Church nor its people, took "possession of every acre of arable land;" nor of "every source of water supply." The whole statement is bathed in falsehood. The testimony before the Judiciary Committee which considered the bill under discussion showed that the right to control the waters of only five streams were given. These five combined would not be larger than the Jordan river, a very medium sized stream. There are in Utah twenty-four counties, in each of which there will average perhaps eight to ten streams—say two hundred all told—nay, say one hundred. Out of this number the provisional government, for the public benefit, gave the use of five streams. Yet Mr. Reed says: "They took possession of every water supply." Comment would be agonizing.

REED. The Mormon Church took possession, under the forms of law, of every acre of arable land.

COMMENT. If they did this where has the arable land taken up by new comers for the last thirty-eight years been obtained? They did not take any save what they required; they hold none that the United States government has not been paid for. Land is being taken up to-day—arable land—in Utah. How then did the Church take possession of every arable acre?

The same falsehood is in the assertion that they took possession of the forests.

But even were all this true, these people did not rob the United States. They were claiming and taking land for themselves as citizens of the United States; claiming the land for their government, which then was at war with the nation —Mexico—to which the land belonged. What becomes of your wild talk in the light of these facts?

REED. That hierarchy has been kept up ever since its organization, inside of the United States and controlling one of its Territories. It is useless to call such a measure as that now before the House an assault upon a religion. It is an assault upon a band of men organized for the purpose of controlling exclusively the territory which belonged to the people of the United States.

COMMENT. You are singularly unfortunate in the selection of terms and phrases. A few moments ago you declared that the "keynote of the situation" was the Mormon "polity." What is the Mormon polity? A church polity, certainly, or there is no point to your keynote; and yet it is not "an assault upon a religion." You call it a "hierarchy," and yet it is not "an assault upon a religion." This "hierarchy," if it exist, exists by virtue of religious tenets which have made the hierarchy what it is. If you depose the men composing this hierarchy the problem is still unsolved, for others will be chosen in their stead. Is this your purpose? Is not the one idea to destroy the principles by which this "hierarchy," as you have called it, exists? If such is not the end in view, then your position is taken in imbecility. If it is your object, then it becomes "an assault upon a religion." Escape the dilemma if you can.

REED. It is an assault upon a band of men organized for the purpose of controlling exclusively the Territory which belonged to the people of the United States.

COMMENT. I ask the reader to pause on the sentence just quoted. It is from the lips of the leader of the Republican party in the National House of Representatives—a party composed of bands "of men organized for the purpose of controlling exclusively the Territory" which belongs to the United States. As a leader of that party he endorses an assault upon a people who, even if he tell the truth concerning them, are doing in a very limited way what he and his party are doing on a magnificent scale. And it is thus he justifies the assault on Mormons. Words are powerless to describe the contempt which such an argument must beget; and to come from such a source!

REED. Polygamy is only one of the incidents of the situation.   *   *   *   It affords me an illustration to show why we can not permit local control to be supreme in that region. You propose to punish a man for violating the laws of the United States with regard to polygamy. What is your practical situation? You bring him before a grand jury. If that grand jury were chosen as grand juries are selected elsewhere, the result would be that the grand jury room would be filled either with men who are committing the same crime, or with those who believe it would be a religious duty for them to commit it if they were worth property enough to sustain themselves in doing so. *If you bring the offender before a jury, you are met by twelve men in a box, the majority of whom must necessarily be men who entirely sympathize with the crime.*   *   *   *   That illustrates one of the difficulties which are in the way of the enforcement of the laws of the United States unless we take some such control of the matter as is proposed in this bill—unless we take hold of it by force of our governing power.

COMMENT. We have it at last. Necessity is the great plea for this legislation. You must cure evil by doing wrong; and the argument is the same; ever necessity, which one writer has termed "the tyrant's devilish plea."

I pass the insinuation that it is a religious duty for every Mormon who has money enough to commit the crime of polygamy, with two observations: First, the insinuation is untrue; second, it would be an excellent condition in other communities if only those persons committed crimes who had sufficient money.

But your reference to the jury system is the point. If your accuracy on all topics were to be judged by your statements on this, you would prove absolutely worthless as an authority. You are a lawyer with politics as a profession. As a lawyer you should understand the law in the case you are trying. The very law to which the bill you were advocating was an amendment provides:

That in any prosecution for bigamy, polygamy or unlawful cohabitation, under any statute of the United States, it shall be sufficient cause of challenge to any person drawn or summoned as a juryman or talesman, first that he is or has been living in the practice of bigamy, polygamy, or unlawful cohabitation with more than one woman,   *   *   *   or second, that he *believes it right* for a man to have more than one living and undivorced wife at the same time, or to live in the practice of cohabiting with more than one woman.

And since it became a law it has been rigorously enforced. No Mormon has been on a grand jury; no Mormon on a petit jury before which a man was being tried for polygamy or unlawful cohabitation. Yet on an unworthy assumption that the reverse was true, you advocated this bill. Only a few moments previous you said that the Mormon "polity" was "the keynote of the situation." Now you hold that the difficulty in the way of punishing crimes is that juries could not, as you stated, but stated untruthfully, be packed by the enemies of the accused. The Supreme Court has decided that an open venire may be issued by United States courts in Utah. The service is made by the United States marshal or his deputies, every one of whom are non-Mormons, some apostates. In spite of these multiplied facts, in spite of your assertion that the Mormon "polity" was the "keynote of the situation," you now urge, as a reason and a necessity for taking control of the Territory by the method proposed in the bill, a condition of affairs in law which does not and did not exist. It is impossible to believe you did not know your statements were untrue. Will you withdraw your support when you learn that you were vilely wrong? Or was your talk purely for cheap theatrical effect?

REED. In addition to the reasons I have given, it is because some time or other we must admit these people to a fellowship in the States, and while we recognize, and I recognize to its fullest extent, the *rights of local self government*, the *right* of the preservation of local institutions, while I admit these *rights* as among the *strongest bulwarks of our liberty*, nevertheless this country must be in the main homogeneous in thought and feeling if it is to be a strong and solid nation.

COMMENT. Again we find the right of local self government affirmed. It was evidently because of your respect for these rights, the "strongest bulwarks of our liberty," that you vote to take them away from a people against whom you can only forge untruths. Clearly you do love the principles. You have no idea how difficult it is to learn, from reading your speech, what you stand upon in your argument against Mormons. Successful issue can be taken on the propositon you advance on the necessity for homogeneity of thought and feeling in a nation so broad, with such varied interests, and so thoroughly impregnated with and wrapped up in the peculiar influences of immediate surroundings; but you are so uncertain and equivocal in all you say, it were an idle task.

And on this testimony (the product of a champion of local self government), on this reasoning, a deliberative body passed a bill to place a community under the heels of petty tyrants and molecular assassians. If nothing better, or worse, can be adduced against this people and their customs, they must stand forever, your reasoning, exhortations and laws notwithstanding.

CHAPTER VI.

HON. J. RANDOLPH TUCKER'S SPEECH.—HIS POSITION IN 1882,
AND IN 1887.—CONSTITUTIONAL OR UNCONSTITUTIONAL.
A HEDGER.—THE POWER OF CONGRESS OVER THE TERRI-
TORIES.—ORIGIN OF PRESENT CLAIMS.— A DEMOCRAT
TAKES THE POSITION WHICH A REPUBLICAN IS ASHAMED
OF.—AN UNDEMOCRATIC DEMOCRAT.—DIRECT AND IN-
DIRECT UNTRUTHS.—A VERSE ON COLONIZATION.—A NEW
POINT ON LANDED RIGHTS.—MR. TUCKER, HENRY GEORGE
AND ANARCHISTS AGREED.—A BAD BREAK ON THE SUB-
JECT OF MONOPOLIES.

IT is singular that a man of wisdom and legal learning
should so soon revolutionize his views, because other men,
as fallible as himself, have declared him to be wrong. To
accept the decision of the United States Supreme Court as final,
would be reasonable; but that a decision by that body is
necessarily and elementarily correct does not follow. You pre-
serve in your bill several features which, in your speech of
1882, you emphatically declared to be flagrant violations of
the Constitution. You objected to the oath formulated in
that bill, yet you beat it out of existence by one you prepare
yourself. You did not like the law of 1882, because it punished
parties by a deprivation of the rights of citizenship without
due process of law, for the reason only that they were suspected of a wrong. But you made an oath that sought to
deprive every man, even those never suspected of wrong-doing
(and that without the most ordinary process of law) of a citizen's
right. Yet you say, save in one point there is nothing "in
conflict" between your position now and the one you held in
1882. You declared in your speech against the Edmunds
bill of March 22, 1882, that the "Constitution follows each
colonist to his new home in the Territories, and shields him
from arbitrary power by whomsoever exercised." And five
years later, you show your faith in this doctrine by devising an
oath which is designed to prevent every Mormon from voting;

but in view of the possibility of this weapon missing fire,
you show your love of the rights of citizenship by giving to
an imported and imposed governor power to appoint all
officers, save a few which are accorded the President of the
United States, thus robbing the colonist of the rights which
the Constitution, as you declare, has promised shall follow
him to his new home; and you place him at the mercy of one
man. In the following words you inveighed against the
commission of five which that bill provided: "Given a board
which is to regulate suffrage, to hold elections, to make
returns thereof, and all this without appeal, and there will be
no difficulty in reaching the conclusion that, for the time being,
140,000 citizens of the United States will be subject to an
autocratic oligarchy as absolute in its authority and capable of
achieving as much unhappiness for its subjects, by the plunder
of their property, the deprivation of their liberties, and the
violation of their Constitutional rights as ever existed among
any people in ancient or modern times." And you ask,
before this, "Is such a law Constitutional?" This Commission, true to your prediction, usurped authority. The
Supreme Court of the United States so decided. But what
have you done in your bill? Destroyed so vicious a Commission?
Ah, no! With wonderful statesmanslike foresight, you have
taken away from them almost entirely all the work which the
Edmunds bill gave them to do, and you have crowned this
effort by continuing indefinitely in power this Commission,
which five years previously you had denounced as unconstitutional. And in one point only, perhaps, we hear you say,
was your position then in conflict with that you occupy now.

But say you, "the Supreme Court has decided these questions." Does that relieve your conscience, or is it any less
your sworn duty to oppose this class of legislation now, if your
convictions are unchanged, than it was before the Supreme
Court rendered that decision. Your opinions and your judgment are your own, as to what is or is not constitutional. An
infinitude of decisions by an infinitude of Supreme Courts
will never swerve from his opposition a man who truly and
conscientiously believes legislation wrong; and while the
court of last resort determines a question as to its legal stand-

ing, it does not, and cannot make right that which is wrong, nor constitutional that which is inherently opposed to the genius of the constitution. It merely ends a legal controversy. It establishes a legal fact. It does not make an eternal truth. The proposition is thus: You were right when you declared the Edmunds bill of 1882 unconstitutional, or you were wrong. If you were right then, you are right still despite the decision of the Supreme Court. If you were wrong then, you had continued wrong though the United States Supreme Court had, times without end, affirmed you to be right.

You hedged. Unmanfully, and without stating that your convictions had undergone a change, you took refuge behind a Supreme Court decision and on its strength would lead all to believe a change of heart had come over you. But if thus you change, no longer boast of being a constitutional lawyer, no longer plead capacity and a life-long study of a sacred instrument. Confess yourself blown about by every wind of doctrine that hies from a republican quarter and throw to the dogs your study of a life. Yet there is but one point of conflict! One point! Yes, but one! The changing, in an hour, and at the point of a personal incentive, in the hope of political preferment, of a life-long protestation of democratic constitutional interpretation, in behalf of one given by rank republicans. De Quincy, I believe, has said, that the characters of men are practically formed at twenty-eight years of age. Mr. Tucker proclaims himself the pitiful exception which establishes the rule.

TUCKER. The Congress shall have power to dispose of and make all needful rules and regulations respecting the territory or other property belonging to the United States. (Constitution United States, Article IV, section 3, clause 2).

I desire to emphasize the words "territory belonging to the United States." It is their territory. It belongs to the United States; to them as copartners.

COMMENT. It is a fact that no democrat can support legislation of this character without forcing himself to accept constitutional interpretations to which democracy is fundamentally opposed, and which are the bulwarks of republican

gospel. How this definition was given to the clause of the
Constitution now quoted, will be seen from the following, the
authority being no less a person than Judge Jeremiah Black.

"Mr. Thaddeus Stevens, the great leader and driver of that day, who
ruled Congress with a sway that was boundless, thought it best in the
beginning to assure his followers that the Constitution had given to
Congress this power over the Territories. To prove it he showed them
the following provision:

'The Congress shall have power to dispose of and make all needful
rules and regulations respecting the territory and other property of the
United States, and nothing in this Constitution shall be construed so as to
prejudice any claims of the United States or of any particular State.'

"That this expressed nothing, and meant nothing, and granted nothing
to Congress, except the power to exercise for the General Government its
purely proprietary rights over the land and goods it possessed, whether
lying within the States or outside of them, was so perfectly manifest that
Mr. Stevens became disgusted with his own argument; he freely expressed
his profound contempt for it, and for all who pretended to believe it.
Having drawn them into it by his glozing speech, his fierce invective
lashed them out again; and he so 'chastised them with the valor of his
tongue,' that they feared to speak of scruples any more. He did not,
because he could not, furnish them any other pretence to stand upon; and
he told them plainly and frankly that he would not stultify himself by
professing to think his measure constitutional. 'This,' said he, 'is legislation outside of the Constitution.' It was passed, and Congress inaugurated
the reign of the thief and the kidnapper by an acknowledged usurpation."

Strange things are from the womb of time. A life-long
professing democrat, from a state that has produced great
men, accepts the interpretation of a constitutional restriction
given by a rank republican who was ashamed of it when he
made it. This is Mr. Tucker's right; but the interpretation is
not democratic; no man can believe it and be a democrat, let
him protest as much as he will.

TUCKER. But there is another and greater constitutional
purpose on the part of this Union in holding that Territory;
and that is to keep it intact for the colonization of *our own
people.*

COMMENT. There is a direct and an indirect untruth in this
allegation. The Constitution, by providing for the enfran-

chisement of aliens and by extending to them all the rights that are accorded to native-born citizens, save one—the right to become President of the United States—made a bid to the inhabitants of all the earth to come and occupy and bless these boundless acres—to win them as long as they willed under precisely such conditions as were imposed upon native-born citizens. As a result, traceable directly to this offer, you are enabled to boast of this as the greatest nation on earth, and of its form of government as the fruit of 1900 years patient and upward development. Take away the immediate and collateral work of enfranchised aliens and what sort of a nation would you have? Thus you state a direct untruth when you assert that the greater constitutional purpose on the part of this Union in holding the territory "is to *keep it intact* as a domain for the *colonization of our own people.*" Advocate this theory in some Irish quarter of New York, or any other State, and note its effect. You dare not.

The indirect untruth is in the inference you would have drawn from the observation preceding the one just criticised, *viz:* that the Mormons who colonized Utah were not our "own people." You should brush up on Mormon pioneer records. You will find Utah to have been pioneered almost exclusively by men born in this country who were the children of parents themselves born of American parents. And for to-day, why Utah has a larger percentage of native born population than any of the northwestern, western and southwestern States and Territories.

TUCKER. It [the land, territory] does not *belong to the first little squad of men who choose to pounce down upon* it and say: "we are monarchs of all we survey, our rights there are none to dispute."

COMMENT. It is very unlikely they will boast their "rights there are none to dispute" while the Tucker species continues to evolve. But if not the first settlers, who, in this country, or where the rights of man have a semblance of recognition, has a right to the land these earliest settlers have blessed by making it habitable? Henry George, consistent with his earnest and oft-expressed belief, denies that priority in land is a right. His is called the gospel of robbery. He is largely denounced as a fanciful and chimerical theorist. Mr. Tucker, in defiance of his avowed principles, asserts the doctrine regarding the Mormons. The assertion is unchallenged. It is applauded. Mr. Tucker is proclaimed a statesman. Queer.

TUCKER. It belongs to the United States, and they have a duty to perform in seeing that this property shall not be monopolized by any class of men or by any Church.

COMMENT. Here again we have the doctrine of Henry George, and of the anarchist, and we have also the customary inferential falsehood; that is, it must be inferred that the land in Utah is monopolized by the Church. If you could prove that fact, if you had just ground to believe this assertion true, would an inferential deduction only have been your method of revealing a truth so damaging to the Mormon Church? Would not you have blazoned it forth in the concentrated eloquence of many generations of eloquent Tuckers? I wot.

But Henry George asserts in substance that all land in the United States is now monopolized by a class. If your argument holds good against the Mormons, then his holds good against the rest of the country, for all land is held under the same conditions: government patents according the titles. If the theory of the anarchist be true, every landowner is, in a degree, a monopolist. If you are right, that land in Utah is monopolized by Mormons, if that is monopoly, how can the anarchist be wrong, since your doctrines accord perfectly? And since you have adopted this line of reasoning, then you will doubtless be able to explain why you do not make legislation on this subject general instead of confining it alone to Utah? I neither affirm nor deny the correctness of these theories. The purpose here is to show with what willingness the country will accept declarations from a legislator on a land subject when it relates to Mormons, and with what alacrity it rejects the same declarations when made by Henry George, or by an anarchist.

TUCKER. They [the United States] have a duty to perform in seeing that this property shall not be monopolized by any special class of men, or by any church.

COMMENT. The United States has no such duty, or if it have, it is a duty more "honored in the breach than in the observance." If what you say be true, you should impeach the officials of government for failing to check monopolies in land; and if there be no laws for the execution of this Constitutional duty, then as a member of several Congresses which failed to enact measures that would give officials power to check these monopolies, you should be impeached for high crimes, for negligence. To what a lofty pinnacle you soar when you assert yourself against Mormons and their religion.

As a lawyer you know that land bought from the United States government, and paid for, belongs to those who have bought and paid for it. They may sell it or give it to whomsoever they please, to be used for whatever purpose they please, if there be no law against such purpose. The United States has no more just power to dispossess them or to deny their right to dispose of the land as shall suit them, than the government of Great Britain has. As chairman of the House Judiciary Committee—which gave birth to the monstrosity you were championing during this speech—as one who, according to your own declaration, not only listened to some thirty hours' of oral argument, but read all you could get on the subject you know there was not a "jot or tittle" of evidence presented before your committee to show that a single foot of the land or "territory" owned by Mormons, or by the Mormon Church, had not been legally bought and paid for by honest money, had not been blessed by the honest toil of Mormons. But, like a pettifogger, you preferred applause before principle. With pettifogging instincts you could make counterfeit utterances, framed to deceive. This you did to win the unmerited support and excite the admiration of your uninformed and prejudiced compatriots of the House, as well as in the hope of commanding the plaudits of an unenlightened and impassioned country.

CHAPTER VII.

TUCKER'S SPEECH CONTINUED.—ANOTHER REASON WHICH IS
LAUGHABLE.—"TERRITORY" AND "TERRITORIES."—CAN
CONGRESS SELL A TERRITORY?—A LOGICAL DEDUCTION
FROM ABSURD REASONING. — "A FELLOW FEELING."—
POWERS OF CONGRESS. — INSUFFERABLE NONSENSE. —
EVEN OF A MORMON.—A WORD ON BELIEF.—INDIFFER-
ENCE TO IT.—A GRAND DICTATOR AND A QUACK STATES-
MAN.—THE GREAT POWER OF BELIEF.

TUCKER. But, sir, there is *another reason* why Congress
has the right to govern the Territories. Congress has
power "to admit new States into this Union." (Constitution United States, Article iv, section. 3, clause one.) The
United States are bound "to guarantee to every State a
republican form of government."

COMMENT. Were not the subject one of so great import,
it would be extremely laughable to note the frantic efforts
you make to justify your ill-chosen position. The section you
quote refers to the admission of States into the Union and
provides, in terms, that Congress shall not be allowed to
admit any State to the Union on any other than a republican
form of government. This clause, section, or article, is
absolutely without reference, the most distant, to the government of the Territories. The attempt to deduce from this,
justification—another reason—for the government of Territories
by Congress, is either a direct intimation that you were
pleading to imbeciles or that you plead like an imbecile. Whatever one may think of the former supposition, I doubt if any
one who reads this argument by you, will challenge the latter
conclusion.

TUCKER. We thus see, that in addition to the *power of
regulating the Territories,*" etc., etc.

COMMENT. Ah! you have caught a woodchuck. The
Constitution says:

"The Congress shall have power to dispose of and make all needful rules and regulations respecting the *territory or other property*, belonging to the United States."

And on this you assert that "in addition to the power of regulating the Territories," etc., Congress shall admit States with certain guarantees. The Constitution speaks of "territory," and you put it "Territories." Is there no difference here? Are you prepared to stake your reputation as a democrat, as a Constitutional lawyer, as a statesman, as a sane individual upon this interpretation? Congress may sell, dispose of (as it does) the territory it owns, as it may of other property, as it may of old cannon, broken down vessels, useless machinery. On this assumption may it sell one of the Territories to a foreign nation, or to an individual? If your position in this respect be well taken, you cannot deny that Congress has such power. The Constitution does not guarantee to every Territory, in direct terms, a republican form of government, though one does read in your speech of 1882 that "the Constitution follows each colonist to his new home in the Territory, and shields him from arbitrary powers, by whomsoever exercised." This was five years ago; but you have changed. You take, on your unequivocal ground, an absolutely reverse view now. It is found in that section of your bill where the people are deprived of the right to elect certain officers and the power to appoint them is placed in the hands of a governor, whom the people know not, to whom this autocrat is in nowise responsible. That is not republicanism. It is despotism, in its vilest form—vilest in that it comes under the guise of freedom, under the cloak and protection of free government. Now if Congress has the right to dispose of the Territories of the United States, if as you hold also by very act, that a republican form of government is not guaranteed a Territory, what is there to prevent Congress from selling the Territory of Utah, *holus bolus*, to some Crœsus, who will crown himself king? Nothing! Under the heavens, if you reason aright, there is nothing! But you say this is absurd! So say I. The absurdity, however, is not in the result deduced, but in the reasoning by which such a deduction becomes possible.

Even if all this be admitted as rational and good Constitutional construction, there arises still another objection. If Congress can regulate "the Territories," as property, it does not follow therefrom that it may govern the people. The people of Utah have bought United States land under conditions so favorable as induced purchase. Congress has just as much right to stop the natural sources of water by which the land is fructified, and because of which the land was purchased, as it has to alter the conditions (those of free government, and the right of the people to inspect the acts of and to hold responsible those who tax and control the taxes) under which the land was first made desirable. This should be good law. But whether good law or not, it is eternal justice. It is the foundation of republican institutions; and the man who would, however slightly, subvert the doctrine, is a traitor to his country, and the fate of traitors should be meted out to him.

The evident purpose of this utterance is to give the impression that a Republican form of government does not now exist in Utah. You also design to give the impression that it is your purpose to secure this boon to the people of Utah, and you go about it in a characteristic way—by depriving them of the last vestige of the form of government your soul yearns to establish. There is a wonderful sympathy between this democrat and the republican from Maine—Reed. They are both clamoring for local self government and freedom. They attempt to secure it by the same methods: by robbing the people of the tattered remnant of self-government that now clothes their suffering bodies. Verily, the lion and the lamb have lain down together. 'Tis Byron writes:

> So well the subject suits his noble mind,
> He brays, the laureat of the long ear'd kind.

TUCKER. Congress then is charged with the duty and vested with the power, by necessary and proper laws, to organize the people of the Territories into distinct communities, *to govern them as shall seem best and proper*, so that they may in due time be fitted to enter the Union as equal States with their older sisters, clothed with a vesture of a Republican form of government. The powers of Congress to govern the Territories thus clearly springs from these clauses of the Constitution by irresistible deduction.

COMMENT. Not by "irresistible deduction," but by insufferable nonsense. The theory has long been that the Territories were government wards—wards not because the people did not possess Constitutional rights, but simply because they were presumably too weak to walk alone. The government was not designed to take from the people in Territories, but to extend a helping hand. That was the theory. But you have changed it; they are not now wards, but slaves, serfs over whom for masters have been placed broken down political hacks, too vile for further use where they were known. A disgrace and a detriment, they are shipped to the Territories, where they assimilate with the people as the hawk assimilates with the barnyard biped—by devouring it. The Territories have thus become the Botany Bay of the country, but most of all has Utah been inflicted with an infectious and scoundrelly set; and it is thus "the Constitution follows each colonist to his new home in the Territory, and shields him from arbitrary power by whomsoever exercised."

The *italics* in the preceding extract are mine. The words are italicised because they are false; because designed, if guided by any judgment whatever in the framing, to convey a false idea. Congress has not the right to do what it "shall deem best and proper" on any subject. If it has, what is the purpose of Constitutional restrictions? You say this to justify a clearly and malignantly unconstitutional attack on a people you hate. It is because Congress has not the power to do as it "shall deem best and proper" in any concern of the country that Tuckers are developed and given seats in Congress. They are placed there to do the behest of the people, with, however, this sworn reservation, that the will of the people must be tolerated only when consistent with that much abused, greatly maligned and sadly ignored instrument, the Constitution of the United States. You frequently deny, as the *Congressional Record* bears witness, the right of Congress to do certain things which many people desire to be done, and which many members of that sacred and awe-inspiring body, the House of Representatives, yearn to have done. Are you

5

in this, as in Supreme Court decisions? Do you surrender your judgment to the will of the majority? But you are not so guided. You have declared, time and again, you would not vote for certain measures. No matter how overwhelming the opposition, you would defend that grand old instrument the Constitution. In the face of this, you assert the right of Congress to do as it "shall deem best and proper" with the Territories. Congress may only, in right, go so far as Constitutional restrictions permit. The limit was more than reached in your villainous production, passed by the House, but which even a Republican Senate, with all its notorious disrespect of Constitutional limitations, could not and did not sanction. It was as a prostitute reproving the wantonness of a woman of reputed virtue.

Tucker. For my own part, Mr. Speaker, I would vote against the bill I have reported if I could be convinced that there was one thing in it which trenches upon the conscience of any man—*even of a Mormon.*

Comment. I doubt if anyone will believe you. It is sad that a man whose life has been devoted to the public service must proclaim his own honesty. But why say: "*Even* of a Mormon!" Impartial men have no use for such expressions. Men, not impartial, who feel themselves so, who announce themselves partial by such utterances, are legally and in sound justice recognized as incompetent to determine a matter fairly. The very expression wherein you profess your candor, damns you by the rank bias it discloses. Truly "the legs of the lame are not equal."

Tucker. I do not care what the Mormon believes. But he must not believe and act upon his belief, if it violates the right of any other man or violates the power of the government and its laws for the peace and good order of society. That is all. I do not object to his saying that he or some other man ought to have two wives or more; but I do not intend to let him or that other man have more than one. If you are not a polygamist in act I do not care what you believe; but I do care very much what you do. When religious belief breaks out into the overt act of polygamy it is time for the civil government to interfere to preserve the peace, purity, and good order of society.

COMMENT. This may be true. Considering your glib sophistries one should perhaps believe you. Let any man read the speech of Senator Call, made in the Senate, February 18, on the infinitely milder bill as it became a law, and escape, if he can, (despite your witless talk to the opposite effect) the conviction that in every line the bill was conceived and framed to affect belief.

Here is a lawyer, a legislator, I presume a logician, who declares himself indifferent to the belief of a people—when every act is but the clothing, the body formed about the silent or the uttered thought of man. As though man could believe and that belief fail to manifest itself. He who says he cares not what a man believes, if he lies, should be discharged from public trust; if he speaks the truth, he should be tried at the bar of humanity as one unworthy respect, as one indifferent to the good of mankind. Men act, work, and strive because of their beliefs. They live so. They cannot live otherwise.

The powers of all just governments end when to every citizen is preserved the right to do as he wills without infringing on the rights of others. Man will think as he chooses. This you cannot prevent; and the loud proclamation that you are willing to accord him this as a blessed boon, is the confession of an arrogant and intolerant spirit, ill-becoming a statesman or a philosopher. When became you grand dictator that you may accord this right and withhold that, as it pleases your self-sufficiency? "I do not object to his saying that he or some other man ought to have two wives or more; but I do not intend to let him or that other man have more than one." Ah, me! We would be great, and with boast and pomp parade our fleeting and tinsel power. We that be so weak. All the Tuckers that ever lived or may yet live cannot down a principle, be it bad or good. If it be bad, in God's hands, they may be instruments in counteracting its evil effects. If it be good, the princple will grind into oblivious powder the whole race of Tuckers, and all others if they strive against it. Yet you say, I will not allow this, but I may consent to that! Great talk for one whose political vestures were even then in tatters and threadbare!

Strange words to come from a man who, by them, widens the rent in his own character.

For the moment, let me again revert to the vague and superficial talk of one who says, he cares not what a man believes. The wise physician, if not too late, endeavors at all times to remove the cause that there may be no disease whatever. Thought, belief, these are the cause of all human action. If men think aright, if they believe aright, it follows, as the night the day, they cannot act a-wrong. Bad acts are the inevitable outcome of bad thoughts and bad faith. But this philospher, this statesman, tells us he cares not for our belief. He, the physician who says: The cause is a matter of perfect indifference to me. Sufficient if I attend the disease which the cause has produced. This the statesman who whipped the American House of Representatives into mob fury, wild, unreasoning, blind. This, he who allowed himself to be carried away by the whirlwind of his passion till his own madness infected all within the sound of his voice. Ah, we have fallen upon remarkable days! And this body passes judgment upon a people whose fault is that believing, that in saying a great belief means something, they are willing that belief shall work out its legitimate results.

CHAPTER VIII.

TUCKER'S SPEECH CONTINUED.—HE FLIES TO HOLY WRIT.—
THE SAVIOR'S WORDS VILELY FALSIFIED.—POLYGAMY CON-
DEMNED, DIVORCE CONCONED.—A SHIFTING FOUNDATION
FOR A DECENT CIVILIZATION.—THE JEWS AS CIVILIZERS.—
WHAT IS A DECENT CIVILIZATION?—MONOGAMY AS A FOUN-
DATION FOR CIVILIZATION IN THE LIGHT OF INFIDEL
GREECE, PAGAN ROME AND REVOLUTIONARY FRANCE.—
WHERE MONOGAMY SPRANG FROM AND WHEN.—PHYSICAL
AND SPIRITUAL DEATH.—POLYGAMY AND CHRIST'S TEACH-
INGS.—A SILENT BIBLE.—THE REDEEMER LIBELED.

BUT you say that polygamy is a crime, and you must needs
fly to Holy Writ to prove it.

TUCKER. Now, Mr. Speaker, that being the power of Congress, what is the duty of Congress to do? What is polygamy? It is a crime by the law of every State in Christendom.
Ever since Christ interpreted the Judaic law and gave it to us
in his own express words, it has not only been a sin against
God, but has been made a crime by every Christian society.
Mark His words:

"For this cause shall a man leave his father and mother and cleave
to his wife, and they twain"—

Not a whole bundle of them,

"They twain shall be one flesh: so then they are no more twain, but
one flesh."

COMMENT. Now you assume the role of theologian. But
a theologian should, above all persons, be sure of his ground
The fact is that, in the words you quote, the Savior did not
make the faintest reference to polygamy. It was not polygamy he was denouncing as a sin in this quotation, but the
sin against God of divorcement—a sin which previls to·day,
the commission of which is "aided and abetted" by the laws
of the State you represent, a sin which I dare you to denounce
in the language you employ against polygamy. Not content
with misrepresenting your fellows, in a mad hatred of Mormons you misrepresent your Savior. Read Matthew xix, and
blush. You cry Christ and sanction divorce! You sustain
divorce and condemn that against which neither the Father nor

the Son has spoken a word! You plead Christianity and yet distort and misapply, for the purpose of enforcing your peculiar ideas, the words of Him who founded the religious system you profess. Were Mormon ever guilty of such base, such corrupt methods, verily he would merit denunciation by mountebanks in politics, quacks in religion—by Tuckers by the score.

But even did the words you quote apply to polygamy, you state what is untrue, when you declare:

TUCKER. Ever since Christ uttered that language, all of the Japhetic races have adopted monogamy as the only foundation of a decent civilization.

COMMENT. The Jews were and are the chosen people of God. Have they not a "decent civilization?" They rejected the Christ and His interpretation of the Judaic law. Was it because of the Savior's words that monogamy became "the only foundation of a decent civilization" among this remarkable race? or are there different foundations for a decent civilization among the different races?

But the Hebrews, being descended from Shem, you may hold to be outside this criticism of your position. The real and underlying point in this utterence by you is that monogamy is the only foundation of a decent civilization, whether among the Japhetic race or not. If that is not your broad ground, then there is absolutely nothing in what you say, since it makes no difference what the race, if the foundation be such that a decent civilization can be built upon it. Your point, therefore, must be that ever since the words you quote from the Savior were uttered by Him, monogamy has been the only foundation of a decent civilization; and it became so because He uttered these words. This must be your point for the reason that it would be childishly absurd to use His name or quote His words, if it were not designed to make Him responsible for your position. Therefore, I ask if the Jews have not a "decent civilization?" Read the history of this most remarkable race, and wherever the blood that courses through their veins has appeared in the nations of the earth, there have followed the blessings of enlightened civilization, as flowers and fruits and abundant harvests follow the April showers and the summer's sun. They are the pioneers of civilization. They have ever been; and through them the children of Japhet, and all others, have been and yet are to be blest. Have not they a "decent civilization?" Having a "decent civilization," did it depend upon the words of the Christ whom they rejected and his enunciation of them now nigh 1900 years ago, even admitting their application against polygamy? Was there not a "decent civilization" among that race when God spoke to, talked with and blessed the father of that race—Abraham, a polygamist? and whom holy men called the friend of God. Was there not something of a "decent civilization"—a foundation for it—among a race that produced a Moses, a law-giver with such inspired insight into the eternally just that all the "glory" of this age, of which you boast so much and so loudly, can devise nothing to supersede the product of that "barbarous age?" How, if monogamy, or Christ's words, as applied by you against polygamy, or both, be the only foundation of a "decent civilization," comes it that the civilization and intelligence of this age cannot go beyond the product of a mind surrounded by "barbarism?" Neither monogomy nor polygamy is the only foundation of a decent civilization; no, nor are the words of Christ as you have quoted, nor is a decent civilization confined to the Japhetic race. A "decent civilization," or any kind of a civilization is only possible where there exists a recognition of a Supreme Being, and civilization exists in degrees, as this principle is accepted in degrees. That profoundly observed, that ardently believed, and whether polygamy, monogamy or celibacy be enjoined, there must be a "decent civilization." Without that, there cannot be a "decent civilization" or any foundation, though you marry but once, a thousand times, or not at all.

But after all is said, what kind of a "civilization" is it that is not "decent?" Oh, the vanity and vexation that comes to one so self-inflated as to imagine he may say what he pleases, and it falls upon the ears of those, insincere and infidel as himself, as holy writ upon the devout believer in the great Catholic Church. A "decent civilization!" As though a civilization could be anything but decent. Nations are civilized in proportion as they have respect for life and cherish principles of virtue. Greece and Rome had a civilization—so-called—founded upon the monogamous system, and so founded in the Japhetic race before, and long before, Christ spoke the words you quote. Do you want to compare their vile and filthy orgies, their disrespect for life, their indifference to children, with the customs that have prevailed among polygamous races? France had such a civilization during the revolution, when the most notorious harlots were placed, nude and shameless, on the highest altars and in the most sacred places, and the people commanded to bow down and adore them. Do you include this, when you say that ever since Christ uttered the words employed by you, "monogamy has been the only foundation of a decent civilization!" France was monogamous then, France is monogamous to-day. Shame on you! Shame! Find, if you can, a parallel to those scenes anywhere in the history of polygamous nations. Yet you can prate about monogamy and a "decent civilization."

Monogamy did not become the rule of civilization among the Japhetic race, (decent or indecent, it matters not to the purpose of this argument) *ever since* the Savior uttered the words you quoted regarding "they twain" and "one flesh." Not until the third century was polygamy condemned, monogamy enjoined. Monogomy was made a rule by a church which every Protestant, by the very nature of his faith, is compelled to hold unworthy and apostate. To the Catholic church we owe monogamy as well as a vast deal of celibacy, and not to Christ. Wise men have long ceased hoping to find in the words of God anything condemnatory of polygamy. But a world which denounces this practice, which names itself civilized, Christian, sanctions divorce and condoles and forgives adultery—two of the most heinous offenses known to the law of God. Divorcement meant to separate that which could not be disjoined without deathly loss. "Neither is the man without the woman, neither the woman without the man in the Lord." Hence, to be divorced was spiritual death, than which even adultery is hardly more fatal. Adultery was punished with physical death. Even the unwillingness of the Savior to condemn the wretched woman caught in the act, has left unaltered the law of God eternally condeming this great sin. "Our civilization," which endures with unaffected complaisance, these violations of God's law, which condones acts that in the times when God was known, meant death spiritually and death physically, now condemns that which not only produces life, but that also which neither the Father nor the Son ever condemned.

The Savior came among a nation that practiced polygamy as of divine permission, if not direction. He denounced murder, theft, lying, blasphemy, hypocrisy, divorcement, adultery, in terms that still speak in trumpet tones. He bade the people to repent and come to him that they might find rest; but in all His recorded words He failed to lay it down as a condition precedent to their receiving His favor, or the blessings promised from obedience to the Gospel, that they must abandon polygamy. He never told them it was obnoxious in the sight of God. Neither did his apostles, nor disciples, speaking by the inspiration of the Father, ever do so. Not from Christ, nor His apostles, nor disciples came the condemnation of polygamy. From the Catholic Church, which to-day enjoins celibacy among a large number of its most honored and devoted believers, in the third century, sprang the opposition to polygamy; and, in wild times, even to marriage of all kinds as degrading and sinful. The result! Well, look out upon your monogamous world, with its licentiousness, divorces, adulteries, prostitution and disease! Look out upon it, and if you can still be proud of what you now boast, then indeed is shame a dead thing among the children of men. It is untrue that the Savior founded monogamy. It is a libel, a fraud to say the Savior, in the words you quote from Him, had any reference to polygamy. A Christian, a man, had never dared speak so falsely of his Redeemer.

CHAPTER IX.

TUCKER'S SPEECH CONTINUED.—THE NUCLEUS OF THE STATE, AND THE CHRISTIAN HOME.—BUNCOMBE.—HISTORY PER-SISTENTLY FALSIFYING.—A CONTRADICTION.—THE GREAT COMMANDMENT.—THE SAVIOR OR MR. TUCKER, WHICH IS RIGHT?—HOMES IN UTAH.—A FEW TUCKER PARADOXES. —A SINGULAR MOTHER DEMANDED.—AN ASSUMPTION.— DEPARTING FROM GOD.—CO-EXISTING MONOGAMY AND POLYGAMY.—WHAT DAVID SAID.—A COUNTERFEIT CHRIS-TIANITY. — A FALSEHOOD NAILED. — DELIBERATE NON-SENSE.

TUCKER. The nucleus of the State is the home of the people. What is the home of the people? The one man and the one woman; *the one man loving supremely none but her; and the woman loving supremely none but her husband.* * * * That is the foundation of your polity; without it there would not be a Christian State in the Union fit to live in. * * * In its loss we lose all which makes modern civilization the glory of our race.

COMMENT. This is simply buncombe. Are there no homes, is there no purity, among polygamous races? Singular, if the home is the basis of the State (as we assert in these times and assert falsely in one sense) if the endurance of the State depends upon the purity of the home, that polygamous nations, which, according to this view, cannot possess pure homes, should be longest lived. How is it that history will persist in falsifying, if there are no homes save monogamous ones?

There are several statements in this paragraph equally irrational and untrue. The Savior, to whom you appealed but a minute before, in reply to a question as to the greatest commandment or duty, declared:

"Thou shalt love the Lord thy God with all thy heart, and with all thy soul, and with all thy mind. This is the first and great command-ment."

You are speaking of the Christian home, and speak of it as the nucleus of the Christian State. The Christian home and the Christian State, to be such, are built upon a supreme love of God, the man being, if necessary, required to leave home, wife and children to follow the Savior. That is the principle upon which the Christian home is built. Yet you can assert that it is founded upon "the one man and the one woman, the one man loving *supremely* her, and the woman loving *supremely none but her husband.*" It is impossible to place the slightest confidence in one who can speak so loosely on matters of such grave significance. Either you are wrong or the Savior is. If the Savior be right, the beginning of welfare to the individual, to the family, and thus to the State is the supreme love of God. This being true, the purity of the home, nor the safety of the State does not depend upon the system of marriage which prevails, but on love of and obedience to God, wherever it may lead. If the Savior be wrong, then your whole argument against polygamy falls, for it rests upon His words. I cannot let you hold Him up to me as an authority one minute and the next have you contradict Him. You have gotten yourself in a bad fix. And thus polygamy is reasoned to be bad. Verily, whom the gods would destroy, they first make mad.

TUCKER. But you may say, "are there no homes in Utah?" yes; but what kind? Homes in which the heart of the husband is divided out and diffused among so many wives that it is lost when it gets to any one, (laughter) the father of a number of distinct sets of children, the wives being mothers each of only one set. What a partnership; what a home in which to rear children! Why gentlemen, that is the basis of a civilization that went out twenty centuries ago, everywhere except in Asia. Ours is the basic principle of the civilization of to-day; theirs of the ancient pre-Christian period of the world's history. With monogamy we are in the lead of progress in the twentieth century of the Christian era. Introduce polygamy and we turn back the dial of our destiny—we obliterate the Christian era, and turn from the light and glory of to-day to the gloom and barbarism of two thousand years ago! That social condition is an Asiatic exotic! ours, a plant of European-American growth. They are as diverse and incompatible as light and darkness. They cannot co-exist, they must be divorced, or one or the other must be extirpated.

The upas tree of polygamy is death to a modern Christian society or to a modern Christian commonwealth.

COMMENT. As you never attempt to reason, it is difficult to reason with you. You simply assert. Therefore it is simply necessary to deny. But let us look at a few of the sentences contained in this remarkable paragraph. Speaking of the homes in Utah and the hearts of husbands being "diffused among so many wives," you say; "the wives being mothers each of only one set" of children. How many sets of children do you expect a Mormon wife to be the mother of?

Again: "That is the basis of a civilization that went out twenty centuries ago everywhere but in Asia?" If this be true how does polygamy happen to be the custom in European Turkey.

Again: "With monogamy we are in the lead of progress in the twentieth century of the Christian era." Though assumed, the fact stated does not prove the progress you boast to be due to monogamy, nor does it prove the progress would not have been greater had polygamy been the social condition of a Christian people.

Again: "That social condition is an Asiatic exotic; ours a plant of European-American growth." Why you have just declared "Ever since Christ uttered that language [they twain shall be one flesh] all of the Japhetic races have adopted monogamy as the only foundation of a decent civilization?" Now you claim it as "a plant of European-American growth." Was not Christ, the founder of your civilization in Asia, a native of Asia? How can anyone place confidence in you who are so flagrantly self-contradictory?

Again: "They [polygamy and monogamy] cannot co-exist; they must be divorced; or one or the other must be extirpated." If you extirpate one or the other, is it not divorced pretty effectually? How can you divorce them without extirpating one? What do you mean by saying, "they must be divorced, *or* one or the other must be extirpated?" You can not explain it, I'll wager.

But granting that all you say here be true, what does it prove? That the Mormons are wrong? That the Asiatic races are astray? Certainly not. You are probably among those who hope for a higher civilization. What may the next century develop? Perhaps that celibacy, as the tendency of the age may seem to indicate, is essential to happiness; perhaps that promiscuous intercourse under the seductive name of free love, as the growth of the spirit of divorce may lead one to fear, is the highest outgrowth of civilization—"the only foundation," in fact, "of a decent civilization." Such a doctrine even now is not without intelligent advocates. Would you, living in such an age, refer to the monogamous system of to-day as the barbarism of a century past? Would such reference on your part make the customs of to-day barbarous? Wise men of all denominations tell us we are departing from the ways of God. Returning to Him, would it follow that we had turned back the "dial of our destiny" to the barbarism of twenty centuries past when men gave up their lives, their all for God and His Holy word? or, would we come once more to "the good old way," rejoicing, as one who, having lost the road, regains the highway? Are you satisfied with your civilization? with its drunkenness, debauchery, adulteries, divorcements, infanticides, abortions, arsons, robberies, murders? with its political corruptions, infidelity and atheism, socialism, anarchy, death? with its shams in religion, bribe-takers in court, quacks in Congress? Oh, the wild boast of madmen! If to return to the olden ages, if to re-enter the "gloom" of 2,000 years ago when the Son of Righteousness gave a glorious and undying light to the children of men, if such a return will save us from the "decent civilization" of this age, then let us pray that the "light and glory of to-day" may die out, be extinguished, never more to return forever. There is no civilization that can bring good where the Omnipotent One and His truths are not. How blindly infatuated are those so swallowed up in self, in their own times, their skin-deep virtues, their heart-deep iniquities, their systems and prejudices, that there is left no good—only "barbarism" in the past! Woe to such. There is much for them to learn, and it will be a bitter learning.

That monogamy and polygamy cannot co-exist is the declaration of imbecility. They do co-exist. They have co-existed for 2,000 years and more. Need more be said. Let me here suggest: When, until undertaken by the Mormons, has polygamy been tried under a full recognition of the divine mission of Christ and the divine authenticity of His teachings? You say they are incompatible. Men say many things. David said all men were liars, and he must have had nineteenth century politicians in his mind's eye at the time. Were it not a fact that polygamy and monogamy have co-existed, how do you know they cannot now, especially under the grand and guiding spirit which the teachings of Christ may impart to them both—that of toleration, patience and a confidence that God works all for the best.

If we accept the statements of many eminent modern divines, we must believe that Christianity is in a very unhealthy state. These divines know whether they judge from signs within or from evidences without. Another proof of the fact is that atheists and infidels, on this statement, accord with the divines. This being true, do you maintain (since they cannot co-exist) that polygamy is destroying Christianity? or would you hold it to be a Christianity, which is counterfeit, reaching the natural and inevitable end of all frauds and forgeries—death? Polygamy might mean death to modern Christianity—as exemplified in its results—but were this an admitted fact, it would simply show that your Christianity, in the wisdom and ecomomy of the Almighty, was unfit to last. As a man who appeals to the authority of Christ, you cannot deny this proposition. If you are right, if polygamy means death to existing Christianity, you should rejoice. If you are wrong, you should—well you should any how—try to keep quiet. How vain we become when prejudice and passion sit where reason and principle should be enthroned. Let me tell you what history teaches: That monogamy and polygamy as they always have, always will continue to co-exist.

TUCKER. Then what? Sit down and let them do as the gentleman from Utah says—"We will work it out one of these days, and if we are wrong we will sink; but you must wait and see how long it will take us."

COMMENT. The gentleman from Utah said his people would sink if they were wrong. You do not deny this. You dare not. It is true by any philosophy, by all philosophy.

He did not say "you must see how long it will take us" to sink if his people were wrong. I quote what he said:

"If the Mormon people are what the popular belief declares them to be, they will destroy themselves more surely, more rapidly, than can be accomplished by any methods to which you dare resort. The effect of immoral practices by communities is such certain, such inevitable decay, that even when all appears best and fairest the death-promoting germs are at work surely and relentlessly undermining, and will bring the whole into that crumbling decay, that putrid ruin, which a beneficent Creator has determined shall be the fate of all that is not builded upon and sustained by the eternal principles of morality. If Mormonism fall, it will fall of its own weight."

And this:

"Time, the great corrector of all evils, will right this wrong, if such it be, and the fiat of the Eternal has already decreed that the last vestige of Mormonism shall be swept away by the peaceful progress of events, if it be not that which God in His wisdom has appointed shall survive as the fittest."

Very different from what you charge him with saying, different because his remark contains a grand and philosophical truth; while what you say is false.

TUCKER. This language seems to make exclusive claim to that Territory [Utah] for the Mormon people.

COMMENT. How often, oh, how often, will you force me to deny the truth of what you say, and to call attention to the absurdity of what you say. No being, the most ingenious, can, with a shadow of reason in his behalf, draw any such idiotic conclusion. It is a wilful and deliberate attempt to make capital in your own behalf by wilful and deliberate nonsense.

CHAPTER X.

TUCKER CONTINUED.—"OUR OWN CHRISTIAN PEOPLE."—A
GENTLE REMINDER.—THE FRIEND OF RELIGIOUS FREE-
DOM DISCOVERED.—THE "JOB" DISCLOSED.—MORE REA-
SONING NEEDED. — THAT POLYGAMOUS STATE. — THE
FALSIFIER IMPALED.—SATANIC EFFRONTERY.—POLYGAMY,
"A VERY SMALL PART OF THE WHOLE BUSINESS."—A
SPEECH HEADED "POLYGAMY" ONLY AN INCIDENT. —
ANOTHER REMINDER OF A PAST ASSERTION.—THE GREAT
UNPARALLELED.—THE STATE OF DESERET.—A REPUDIATOR
REPUDIATED.

TUCKER. Why, sir, that is our Territory, our domain for the homes of *our own Christian people to dwell in.*

COMMENT. You have said of the land owned by Mormons in Utah: "It does not belong to the first little squad of men who choose to pounce down upon it and say 'we are monarchs of all we survey; our rights there are none to dispute.'" Therefore, it does not belong to the first Mormon settlers. You have said in substance that there are no Christian homes in Utah, because the Christian home consists of one man and but one wife who loves "supremely none but her husband," while in the homes in Utah the heart of the husband is "divided out and diffused among so many wives that it is lost when it gets to [any one." (How the heart can get to any woman when it is lost before it gets there is one of those paradoxes which only a Tucker can explain.) And now you say this domain is "ours," "for the home of our own Christian people to dwell in." What conclusion is a Mormon to draw from these declarations? That the land bought, redeemed and paid for by him is not his; that he is not a Christian, and that it is proper for Christians to drive him out, rob him, and dwell in the land he now occupies. This is the only deduction possible. Posing as a Christian champion, you advocate the doctrine of robbing Mormons. You urge, jamb through Congress a bill designed to justify this robbery; you announce the intention in your speech, and yet you say of the Mormon: "I would protect him with as much care as I would protect one of any other religion;" and you will say a little later: "If there is any-body in the world that is bound to be a friend of religious freedom, it is a man born in the commonwealth of old Virginia." You were born in old Virginia. Yet you, in the face of these declarations, justify the robbery of Mor-mons, because you say they are not Christians—because of their religion. One can now understand why you dared not challenge Mr. Bennett, of North Carolina, when he declared in his speech, just before you, that this bill was "a job." You did not deny the charge; and by the words of your mouth, you proved that he had spoken the truth. This is the champion of Christianity and of the Christian home.

TUCKER. Why, sir, that is our Territory, our domain for the homes of *our own Christian* people to dwell in.

COMMENT. It has already been shown that the Constitu·tion of the United States has made a world-wide bid to the poor and the rich of all nations to come hither and take these lands. But you touch another point here. As a Constitu-tional lawyer of profound erudition you will kindly give your authority for the assertion that this land is reserved either for "our own people" or "our own Christian people to dwell in." You have given article, section and clause with astonishing glibness heretofore. Why not do it now? You cannot. The Constitution knows no religion. You simply make yourself supremely contemptible in the way you proceed. Even did the Constitution justify you in your falsehoods, you would then, to make good the point, be required to prove first that the Mormons were not "our own" people, and then that they were not a "Christian" people, for whom these lands are reserved.

TUCKER. We want that [Utah] as one of the States of this Union. And why does it not come in? Why does it, with 180,000 still, as it has for forty years stood, stand as a province of the Union and not as a State of the Union? Be-cause there are 150,000 Mormons there that would perpetuate polygamy as an institution of their society.

6

COMMENT. That is false. Again and again, the people of Utah have come to Congress and, with a fair and republican constitution, built upon those of more advanced States, begged to be admitted as a State. Their petitions have been ignored.

How do you know the Mormon people would perpetuatè polygamy? Has Congress asked them? Have they ever been given a chance to enter as a State on a constitution which would prohibit forever the practice or countenance of polygamy? You cannot tell what the Mormons will do until you have given them a chance.

Reader let me tell you of this man, who condemns the Mormons because Utah is not a State. When he had closed the two hours' debate on this bill, and had moved the previous question, to cut off all amendments and all ₍possibility of further debate, Mr. Scott, a representative of Pennsylvania, pleaded three times to have the privilege of reading to the House, for its information, an amendment which he had prepared to the bill. Mr. Tucker, had supreme command of the time of the House; he could have permitted this amehdment to be discussed, to be read. He positively declined to hear it himself or permit the House to hear it. What was that amendment? I give it here:

"That this act shall not take effect till six months after its approval by the President, and there shall be an election held in the several precincts o f
· said Territory, on the third Monday in March, 1887, at which the qualified electors of the said Territory may elect, from each legislative district, double the number of delegates they are entitled to elect of councilors and representatives to the Legislative Assembly of said Territory, and the delegates so elected shall meet at Salt Lake City, on the first Monday of April, 1887, at 12 o'clock, noon, and shall form a constitutional convention, and if said convention shall form and adopt a constitution, republican in form, and *which shall prohibit polygamy in said State,* and the same shall be ratified by a majority of the votes cast by the qualified electors at an election to be held for that purpose in the several precincts of that Territory, on the first Monday of June, 1887; then the provisions of this act shall continue to remain inoperative until such constitution shall be presented in the usual manner and acted on by Congress. The elections herein provided for, are to be held, conducted and returns thereof

made in the manner now provided by law for the holding of elections for county and precinct officers in said Territory, and all acts and parts of acts in conflict with the provisions of this section shall and will remain inoperative until the expiration of said six months, and in the case of the adoption and ratification of said constitution as hereinbefore provided, the said provisions shall remain inoperative until action on said constitution by Congress."

And yet this man has the satanic effrontery to charge that Utah is a province and has been for forty years, when she might have been a State, because the people of Utah would perpetuate polygamy as an institution in their society.

TUCKER. Why do not other people go there? Why, how can people go there when it is occupied by this number [150,000] of a polygamous church who insist on making it a polygamous State?

COMMENT. This needs no comment when it is stated by you that there are in Utah 180,000 people, and that 150,000 of this number want to make a polygamous State. How come this 30,000 here who do not want polygamy? The testimony before your committtee showed that there were in Utah perhaps 2,500 polygamists out of a population of 180,000. Yet you assert that 150,000 would continue polygamy as an institution in Utah; and ask why people do not go to Utah. It is a fair exhibit of the pitiful character of your arguments. I blush for you. A Mormon blushes for you. Think of it!

TUCKER. Why, sir, what is this Mormonism? Is it merely polygamy? Are we dealing with the individual crime of the individual man? Not at all; or only incidentally. *That is a very small part of the whole business.*

COMMENT. Indeed. I am reviewing your speech as published in the *Congressional Record*, or from it, in ¡pamphlet form, after you had revised it. Do you head this speech "Mormonism," or give it some title that will embrace the whole subject? No. You head it "POLYGAMY;" to give out the impression that this is the burden of your remarks, and then you refer to it as "merely polygamy," only "an incident." There is not another practice peculiar to the Mormon religion which the law can touch, or for which any person can be punished; and in this bill you do not attempt to make a crime of anything else that affects only the Mormons. Yet, speaking of polygamy as merely an incident, you would convey the impression that you proposed to deal with other crimes existing among the Mormons and that this polygamy was but an insignificant incident.

But you have also said: "That the nucleus of the State is the home of the people." That the home consists of one man and one wife each supremely loving the other; that "as is the family, so will be the State." That as the Mormons are polygamous they have no such homes, and that as their practice is fundamentally at war with that of your Christian homes, they therefore are at war against the State; they therefore are traitors to the State, as the home of the one man and the one woman each loving supremely the other "is the foundation of your [national] polity." And now you assert that it is "only an incident;" that it "is a very small part of the whole business." I leave you in the hole you provided for yourself.

TUCKER. Any man that will look into the history of this thing [Mormonism] will see that, as the gentleman from Utah said to-day, or said to-day in substance, "every Mormon member of a church is bound by his fidelity to the church to see that the State is run in favor of the Lord."

COMMENT. You are certainly the great unparalleled. The gentleman from Utah, Mr. Caine, denied that he made any such assertion. His denial is good. What you attribute to him is not to be found in his speech because he never uttered it. This is what he did say:

"They [the Mormons] believed and taught then, as they believe and teach to-day, that the Government of the United States was founded by men who were inspired of God. It mattered not what they had suffered at the hands of lawless men, or wherein those in authority had failed to do their duty, the Mormon religion imposed upon those who accepted the faith the sacred obligation of supporting, defending, and aggrandizing that Government, the establishment of which was but part of the latter-day dispensation."

How does this fact compare with your charge against him? But even were it as you say, what then? Note the position into which your witless verbiage forces you. We have heard you, only a few minutes ago, appealing to the word of God to support you in denouncing polygamy. Upon that argument you rested this part of your case. Now you complain that it is the sworn duty of every Mormon to run the State "in favor of the Lord." You have declared that the domain of the United States, is reserved for habitation by a Christian people. The highest aim of a Christian people is to serve the Lord. Now, having found a people who, as you assert, are bound by their "fidelity to the Church to see that the State is run in the interest of the Lord," you are beside yourself at their iniquity. You must pass legislation that will not only prevent them dwelling in the domain reserved for them to dwell in, but destroy them as a community. The shifts of the quack to make both ends of an argument meet are pitiful indeed.

TUCKER. In their constitution they [the Mormons in 1849] set up their authority as of the Lord.

COMMENT. As a Christian you ought to look upon that as pretty good authority. But you do not even stop to dispute this claim.

TUCKER. In their constitution they set up their authority as of the Lord, in which they said that they themselves must be the government of that Territory, "until the Congress of the United States shall otherwise provide for the government of the Territory, hereafter named and described, by admitting us into the Union!" that is to say, they claimed to be an independent State of Deseret until they were admitted into the Union, as a free State inside the Union. * * * This was a clear and distinct usurpation of authority. * * * By this act of the Mormon government the power of Congress was utterly repudiated.

COMMENT. Is this reason? If what you here declare be true, then what you deduce is false. This was in 1849—thirty-eight years ago. Recently you inquired with that candor which is a painful characteristic with you: "Why does it [Utah] still, as for forty years it has stood, stand as a province of the Union and not as a State in the Union," and you answer that it is because there are 150,000 Mormons who would perpetuate polygamy as an institution. According to this, the Mormons might have had statehood the very year they reached Utah, then a country belonging to Mexico, and two years before they repudiated the authority of Congress. Has Congress, all these years, been willing to admit a people which repudiates its authority? How can you be believed?

If, in the constitution of the Provisional Government of the State of Deseret, it was provided the people there, in that country, and not the people somewhere else, should control affairs until Congress would admit Deseret or Utah, or that section of country, as a State into the Union, that was not a repudiation of the authority of Congress. Was not the very reference to the Congress in this connection a recognition of the right of that body to admit what is now Utah as a State, or to deny the admission? It must occur to all persons of sense that a man who would reason as you have done is beside himself— self-infatuated, self-blinded. If there has been no better sense, or display of it, at the bottom of the assaults on Mormonism, it is cause for little wonder that all attacks heretofore have proven rank failures.

One question may be pertinent. When Congress saw fit to frame for Utah a Territorial form of government, did the Mormons, or the Mormon Priesthood ever oppose its establishment? Is there any record of opposition? Has it ever been charged that such establishment was resisted because statehood was not offered? A man who would pass as impartial and a competent judge, should be sure that his position is safe. It was not unnatural, nor does it give the slightest evidence of bad faith or repudiation of the national government, that the Mormons should establish a government on the fundamental principles of the nation—the right of the governed to say by whom and how they shall be governed. Believing that there still remained a faith in this principle among the American people, these Mormons framed such a government, to fill a needful purpose, to last until the Congress of the United States, mentioned by name by this people in their constitution, should, in its wisdom, deem them worthy of an enlarged exercise of the powers they claimed a right, even then, as American citizens, to exercise in a limited degree. It is the consummation of political corruption, of

nineteenth century quackism, for an American Congressman to charge as repudiation an act that could only have
been conceived where republican principles were warm in
the hearts of the people. They have been driven again and
again from homes; denied restitution and protection, wan-
dered into desolate wilds; worked for years in suffering; made
a home for broken down government hacks and political
tramps and scoundrels, who would have ridden them to
death had they been traitors, who have heaped obloquy upon
them, who have called them whoremasters, perjurers, assas-
sins, who have called their wives prostitutes, and who rejoice in designating their children bastards; and as a consummation, a political quack, a life-long sham, a son of a
State dishonored in his person, rises in the American Congress
and charges this long-suffering and enduring people with
repudiating Congress. This is the consummation of humilia-
tion—to be denounced at such hands. What was to prevent
the Mormon people openly and avowedly repudiating the
authority of the United States in 1847, or on till 1860 or 1865?
Was it repudiation that caused the driven and despoiled
children of a free government to plant the stars and stripes
on Mexican Territory? Bah! What was to prevent them
denying the right of Congress to form a Territorial government here? There were no troops within a thousand miles.
Ah me! vain is reason to wilful fools and blinded bigots.

CHAPTER XI.

TUCKER CONTINUED-—A CORPORATION ALREADY DEAD TO
BE MADE "DEADER."—THE DOGBERRY REVEALED.—HE
WANDERS INTO THE PAST.—PROFOUND SECRETS WHICH
ARE NOT SECRETS. — ANOTHER DILEMMA. — MORMON
RULES THAT ARE UNKNOWN, YET WHICH MR. TUCKER
HAD IN EVIDENCE BEFORE HIS COMMITTEE.—A RICH
CHURCH DISCOVERED.—THE JOB AGAIN.—DISESTABLISHED
AND DISORGANIZED, A VITAL DISTINCTION.—THE MYS-
TERIES OF RELIGION.—THE OLD STORY OF DANGER TO
THE STATE.—"WE BE FREE."

TUCKER. Now I say * * * that what the "State
of Deseret" did after it became a Territory of the
United States, and after the Organic Act was passed,
was absolutely null and void. The incorporation of the
Church, therefore, has no sound foundation, and has had none
from the beginning. Afterward they incorporated the Perpetual Emigrating Fund Society, and made it an annex to the
Church.

COMMENT. Were this all, 'twere well with you. But when
the Territorial Legislature, acting under the Organic Act,
.adopted the work of the Assembly of the Provisional Government of the State of Deseret, how then? and when these acts
of the Territorial Assembly remain valid till repudiated by
Congress, what is there left of your glib talk? If they are
null and void, why do you now undertake to invalidate that
which has no standing or existence in law? The very arguments you make to justify the passage of your bill, prove the
bill to be needless. If the incorporations are dead, null and
void, there needs no act to make them so. If the act be
necessary to make them invalid, then they have a genuine and
actual existence that can only be estopped by Congressional
enactment. But dead or alive, void or valid, this Dogberry has
again written himself down an ass.

TUCKER. I saw acts of the Assembly in which they gave
a whole valley, the Valley of Cache, to Brigham Young, in

trust for the Church; * * * acts showing that all the legislation of the civil power was in the direction of building up the Kingdom of the Lord, as it was represented in the Church of Jesus Christ of Latter-day Saints.

COMMENT. Is that why you advocated a bill against polygamy? But the bill is for the present and for the future; not for the past; that you cannot touch. Even were this act wrong then, what does it signify now? It is not the first time in the world's history that such things have been done. I have already had occasion to show the vanity of one who appeals to the Lord in one instance because it agrees with him, but who, in the next, has the most decided objections to Mormons doing the same thing.

What you should have done—what would have become a statesman who is legislating for existing evils—was to show that the Mormon Church *to-day* owns land that has not been paid for to the government, that has not been formally and properly entered. You say you listened to thirty hours of oral argument on the subject of Mormonism, and read all you could obtain. Did you ever hear that the general government had not been paid for this land? I have read all the arguments made before your committee. I know the charge was not made. If you are to legislate on church organizations, because of disagreeable things you may discover in their past history, you will have opened an inexhaustible field, and the Mormon Church, being the youngest, will have the least iniquity to account for. If this is the outcome of your legal training, if it effects all lawyers alike, one can understand why the Knights of Labor are fundamentally opposed to the admission into their societies of a lawyer. If, however, you could persuade the Knights to read your argument now under review, you might escape the most distant suspicion of being a lawyer.

TUCKER. They have their secret services in the Endowment House, where oaths are taken that never get beyond its threshold.

COMMENT. I will call you truthful if you can prove this. If such oaths were taken, there would also be administered an oath forbidding their discovery. If these oaths never get beyond the threshold of the Endowment House, how do you know they are taken? I have heard Miss Kate Field, who presumably furnished the testimony on the subject presented before your committee, read what she said were the Endowment House oaths—all of them, I understand. If these oaths are true, they were furnished by persons foresworn and confessed oath-breakers. Is this the character of testimony on which statesmen and legislators adjudge a community guilty? Did these oath-breakers, or liars, for they must be one or the other, ever assert there remained other oaths which even they dared not divulge? Never.

TUCKER. The power of the hierarchy is complete and absolute, but the rules by which it acts are hidden from the eyes of men.

COMMENT. This is on a par with the above. For a man who listened to thirty hours' oral argument on the subject, and read so much, and who never heard or read such a statement, it comes as near being deliberate slander as can well be conceived. The evidence before your committee during the inquiry into this subject, showed that the rules for guidance among Mormons were contained in the Book of Doctrine and Covenants. That book was introduced in testimony, and from it extracts were read by R. N. Baskin, who has for years been striving to bring the people of Utah into political bondage. It was introduced as a book containing the rules by which the "hierarchy" obtained its power; it was acknowledged by Mormons present as containing the rules, and all the rules by which they were guided; it was introduced with a view to doing harm to the Mormon character, and in the face of this fact, you dare to say "The rules by which it [the hierarchy] acts are hidden from the eyes of men." Nay, more: It was in testimony that this very work, the Doctrine and Covenants, was kept in the Congressional Library for public inspection, and the copy used by Mr. Baskin was conceded by the Mormons, and their representatives present, to be authentic.

TUCKER. They have accumulated property to a very large amount—to how large an amount we know not.

COMMENT. And is this the cause for the assault? Why then, how about polygamy? Mr. Bennett, in the debate on January 12, deliberately characterized the endeavor to pass this measure as "a job." It is not so reported in his speech, but he did nevertheless, make the charge, and you failed either to deny, or challenge that allegation. Was it because the Mormons "have accumulated property to a very large amount—to how large an amount we know not"--that you wanted to pass this measure, which Judge R. T. Bennett characterized as "a job?" That you had in this bill arranged for an interminable lawsuit on which lawyers might feed and fatten?

TUCKER. The great attack upon this bill is made upon that provision of it which disestablishes the Church—disin-corporates it. That is proposed by this bill to be done, Mr. Speaker, because I believe that, as long as that *organized power* of the Church continues, so long will every member of that Church be under its control, and thus make the power of the State simply the power of the Church.

COMMENT. If you could "disorganize" the Church there would be no need to disestablish or disincorporate it. The disorganization would accomplish all ends. Foolishly you mix the words, as you will see with a moment's thought. Though you disestablish and disincorporate the Church it will remain organized, and since disorganization is the evident purpose (for you object to its *organized power*) you prove yourself a very vain and very silly man. The members of the Church only can disorganize it. Your laws to accomplish that end are just about as wise as the attempts of a man to kick the moon out of place.

But polygamy—though only an incident—was the first and consuming crime at which this bill was aimed. Polygamy was unchristian, and would turn back the "dial of our destiny" to the "gloom" and "barbarism" of 2000 years ago, which produced the greatest, purest, best being that ever trod the earth—whether as man or God— the Great Exemplar of all enlightened times. To such barbarism. Then we find a rich Church, how rich we know not, but rich enough, according to one de-bater, to prompt an unspotted son of Virginia to crowd through "a job." And then we come to the marrow of the bone—always scouted at, pooh poohed and vehemently denied—the thing to be destroyed is Mormonism; and because it wields power. We have already learned that you do not care for belief; and that you object *only to the overt act of polygamy*, but now we find you consistently inconsistent, (in the position that is the sure portion of those who love falsehood and vain applause better than truth and manliness) repudiating yourself. The Mormon belief makes the Mormon Church strong; and you would destroy the Church in the hope that the belief may cure itself. The quack will advertise himself, gild him with fame and cover him with collegiate diplomas as you may. I have already discussed this proposition—the temporal effect of every living religion—in the review of Mr. Reed's argument. It need not be repeated. This I will say: As soon as a religion has lost all influence on temporal affairs, so soon it is dead. All the embalming that human ingenuity may provide cannot pre-serve it from putridity and fitting dissolution. If it live, it will have temporal effects; and those effects will reach the civil government, despite all the shams, and quacks, and mounte-banks, and pettifoggers that can be assembled in Congress, or in the world, and despite the legislation of all governments from the greatest and freest to the least and most despotic. Men live, Carlysle says, by believing something. No Congress, or Parliament ever existed that could legislate out of the heart of man a deep, living belief. While that belief lasts, it will "or-ganize," and that organization will be strong, though you try to kill it by oceans of acts and speeches. Men who are advocates of such methods as you propose here, are to legislation what the maker of a cure-all pill is to humanity—a rank, unmitigated fraud. We may say as we please, but the restraining influence of the Catholic religion, despite our hatred of it, has been a God-send to many blatherskites before the invention of this latest edition of the Tucker family. The man who would seek to destroy the power of a religion which, in any degree, restrains men, or in any manner, works for good, can only be likened to the idiot who sawed off from the tree the limb on which he sat. He was rewarded with a broken neck.

TUCKER. When religion veils itself in mystery and organizes its power over its individual members under the dread claim of a divine commission to direct the actions, and bind the consciences of men; when it accumulates great wealth, and thus, through superstitious reverence, and by the influence which concentrated and corporate wealth always acquires, wields power over civil affairs; such an ecclesiastic organism is a menace to the civil power, and becomes dangerous to the liberty of the people and to the peace and good order of society.

COMMENT. When does religion do this? Never. Men do it. There are political quacks and charlatans who do it, notably in the arguments in favor of this bill, if we substitute for "divine commission" the words "divine reason."

If you mean by this, and of course you do, that such is the aim of, such the end attained by the Mormon Church, I give you, as a Mormon, the "lie as deep as to the lungs." I dare you to prove it. Men have said this and more of the Catholic Church. They have been whipped by reason for their pains. They have passed away into a silence unfathomable, and the mysteries of religion and the ecclesiastical organizations they denounced, are still mysteries and controlling powers among men.

And you object to the mystery with which religion veils itself because it becomes " a menace to the civil power," and dangerous to the liberty of the people. You pose for a Christian, or you have, on your own word, no rights here. This land is reserved, we have heard you say, for Christian people to dwell in, and of course you are one of them, or you should be cast out. Can you unwrap the mystery that enshrouds the Godhead? Can you follow, explain, pin down, anatomize the operations of the Holy Ghost? Can you disentangle the skein of faith, and the principle on wh'ch it works among men? Is there a single point connected with your belief as a Christian that, pushed to its human limits, will not lose itself deep and dark in unfathomable and boundless mystery? Unclean are the lips that can cry Christianity, bad the heart that appeals to Christ and yet protests that religion veiled in mystery is a "menace to the civil power," "dangerous to the liberty of the people." There was one of old, learned even as thou, with all thy getting, and blessed withal with the day star of inspiration, who wrote: "Great is the mystery of Godliness;" and one of old, of the "barbarism" and "gloom" of 2000 years ago, the blessed Exemplar, who said it was blessed to believe and see, but a greater blessing to believe and not to see; that He had many things to say that they then could not understand; that only by faith all things were possible. And the Jews, who could not understand Him, had Him crucified because His religion was veiled in mystery and because it was a "menace to the civil power," and a danger to the liberty of people. "We be free!" they cried.

You dangle daintily on a dangerous gulf. The years roll about you. Speak some true, some serious farewell word ere they engulf you forever, or be wise and—silent. Oblivion! It will come to you. It comes to all save those that speak the truth. For the rest, but a groan and all is passed—silence, eternal, unfathomable. The true word only lives forever; the true act alone endures for always.

CHAPTER XII.

TUCKER CONTINUED.—A NEW QUESTION.—A GREATER THAN DIANA OF THE EPHESIANS.—THE OLD STORY OF CHURCH AND STATE WITH A SINGULAR VARIATION.—WISER THAN THE BUILDER OF HEAVEN AND EARTH.—UNDISGUISED ATHEISM. —A QUESTION AND AN ANSWER WHICH NAILS A PREVIOUS UNTRUTH.—ANOTHER QUERY AND ANOTHER REPLY.—A WILFUL DECEPTION—REMINDERS IN SEVERAL DIRECTIONS. —A BAD BOX.—FREEDOM OF WORSHIP.—A PARTNERSHIP. —THE CHURCH TOO SACRED.—THE DEDUCTIONS THAT ARE NOT WANTED.

TUCKER. The question for the committee was this: Is it not public policy to disestablish the Church, to put it on the same basis with all other churches, and by dissolving the corporation of the Church leave its members as citizens free from this corporate ecclesiastical authority to act as their judgments should dictate in civil affairs; to free the man from corporate shackles and leave him to independent action as a citizen of the State.

COMMENT. Here, again, we have the expressed determination to destroy the organization of the Mormon Church. This was called a bill against polygamy. On this cry it was approved by the country. But its wily manager, with all his legal cunning, in the heat of debate, and lashed by the consciousness of a traitors' and turn-coat's shame, cannot disguise his real intent, but discovers that it is the destruction of the Mormon Church he desires. What else can this language mean? I call attention again to the fact that David says all men are liars, and add, that liars, of all people should have good memories. Otherwise they had better tell the truth. The assumption in this paragraph that the members of the Mormon Church are not free to act as they choose is one of the cute methods common to tricksters who mistake sophistry for reason, and silence for conviction. Imagine a sane man telling one who can think, that he must do so; imagine him telling one who, by nature, lacks the power for the continued thought necessary to reach sound conclusions, that he must act for himself, think and judge for himself! But imbecile as this is, it is God-like in its wisdom to the rank idiocy of him who imagines he can make reasoners of men by disestablishing their church. Here indeed, may we cry, "Oh reason! thou hast fled to brutish beasts." Great was Diana of the Ephesians, but greater Tucker of Virginia, for he, by legislative enactment, will take the shackle from the Mormon mind, and set the enthralled reason at God-like liberty. Say not the gods no more do visit the earth!

TUCKER. As to the power of the Church to accumulate property and mingle itself too much with the temporalities of this world, we know that that will corrupt the church, and that when the church is corrupted, it will corrupt the state.

COMMENT. The old adage runs: "Give a fool rope enough and he will hang himself." Here we have it exemplified anew. Do you forget that you have already declared:

"The nucleus of the state is the home of the people. What is the home of the people? The one man and the one woman; the one man loving supremely none but her, and the woman loving none supremely but her husband. Thank God there are such homes yet in this great land which He has given to us and our posterity. That is the foundation of your polity; without it there would not be a Christian State in the Union that would be fit to live in. The family is the germ of society. As is the family, so will be the state.

Of these two opposing statements, which are we to accept? Does the purity of the state depend on the home with one wife, or on the freedom of the church from temporal affairs? All your cheap talk about the home and one wife, and the children and the state, becomes, by this later enunciation of fundamental principle, froth and buncombe. You also forget, that but a brief space before (after having appealed to the word of the Lord to bolster up your assault on polygamy) you became furious because the Mormons are required by their fidelity to run the state in favor of the Lord. This time, like the clown in the circus, you perform a grand double summersault, and returning to your first love, tremble lest the church should become corrupt, and the state suffer thereby. The church, lest it should be contaminated, must be removed to a sphere where its power to do harm becomes as limited as its capacity for doing good; it must cease to be either of earthly or of heavenly use, lest it might do harm; *i. e.:* it must cease to exist. Our statesman's wisdom exceeds that of the Almighty Himself and the Son of Man; for while God designed His Gospel to go among the children of men and lift them from the errors of their ways, our hero would save the church at the expense of the inhabitants of the earth. What more can Atheism ask? This from a Christian! one who appeals to the Divine lawgiver! Can words express the contempt, the deep, unutterable contempt, which wise men and true must feel for one like this?

Just mark the following question and answer:

MR. WARNER, of Ohio. Will you please state just here, for the information of the House, whether the Mormon Church *still owns those lands* which you say were granted by the State of Deseret?

MR. TUCKER. *Yes, Sir.* I have already stated in the report, and I state now, that after the power of the Territory got into the hands of the United States, after Brigham Young was "disestablished" as governor, by President Buchanan, the Legislature *revoked a great many of those grants of property to the Church*, but the establishment of the Church was afterwards confirmed by the Territory of Utah, at some time before 1860.

COMMENT. In the last two lines of this answer you assert what proves you to have told a wilful untruth before. You have previously said that the church incorporation was null and void because organized by the state of Deseret after the passage of the act organizing the Territory. You deliberately omitted in that connection to state what you now acknowledge: that the establishment of the church was afterwards confirmed by the Territorial Legislature. You did not state it then because it would have destroyed your point. Why, in 1882 you said, speaking against the Edmunds bill passed that year:

"It appears that the governor and Legislative Asssembly of Utah, by an act passed January 19, 1855, adopted and re-enacted an ordinance passed by the provisional government of Deseret February 8, 1851, by which Mormonism with its polygamous rites was legalized in that Territory.

MR. PETERS. Is the title to their Church property derived from any other source than the Territorial act?

MR. TUCKER. They may have obtained some of their property from individuals. I think it is the fact that they have done so. I will come to that point in a moment, to show the reason for one feature of this bill.

COMMENT. But you never come to the point—wisely drop it there. For one who boasted he had read all he could get on the subject and listened to thirty hours oral argument, for one supposed to give ample reason, and be in possession of sufficent proof to justify his urging such a measure through the House in mad haste, you have a very faulty memory— though excellent enough when it is convenient. The question itself is a painful exhibition of ignorance. As though a Territorial government could convey to any person or set of persons any of the domain of the United States. About twenty minutes before you answered Mr. Peters' question, you were quoting from the Constitution:

"Congress shall have power to dispose of and make all needful rules and regulations respecting the Territory or other property belonging to the United States."

You have said: "It belongs to the United States," not "to the first little squad of men who choose to pounce down upon it;" "that is our territory, our domain for the homes of our own Christian people to dwell in." And so on. You hold Congress can do as it "shall deem best and proper" with this land, this territory, and yet, when a very foolish question is asked, with characteristic insincerity you hedge and say you believe so and so. You know that the Territory could not give an acre of the land. You knew that Congress had never given the church a rod. You knew that if the church held so much as a single foot which had not been properly entered and paid for, a horde of adventurers, inspired by your Christian possession theory, would pounce upon it, and that such men as J. Randolph Tucker would proclaim the dismal fact to the ends of the earth through the medium of the *Congressional Record* and a speech held for revision. What a base, cowardly wretch untruth and evil purpose make of an animal originally designed for man.

TUCKER. We propose to enact in the eighteenth section of this bill that the Mormon Church and all other churches shall have the right to worship God according to the dictates of their own conscience.

COMMENT. Your method of stating untruths without stating them—leaving the inference certainly to be drawn—manifests itself perpetually. You know, if you know anything about the subject, that there has never been hindrance in Utah to any person worshipping God as he wills. You would, however, by this cheap utterance, bolster up a previously deducable untruth, that religious toleration was a dead thing in Utah. This, too, when the men who have abused the Mormons in your hearing live, and live well in Utah; when ministers, whose flocks are in Utah, make periodical pilgrimages east to gather in stray pence by denouncing Mormons as the scum of the universe. In the face of these notorious facts, you would insinuate that freedom of worship was not tolerated in Utah.

TUCKER. In my judgment there can be no such partnership as that [the plan proposed by the Senate bill that the United States appoint thirteen trustees to control the Mormon Church]. I hold the Church of God too sacred for any such partnership. There can be no partnership, as there is no concord between Christ and Belial. Let church and state stand apart.

COMMENT. Once more we perceive a burning affection for the Church. The Church is too sacred for earth—that is the substance; and the God of Heaven, when he established it here, made one of those mistakes which but one Tucker in a life-time discovers. There must be a divorcement. Divorcement means death. If the Church has no temporal effect, it can have no existence. You object to it having temporal weight. You would save the Church by killing it. The Church must die that it may live. Such is your reasoning. It is too sacred for the earth, and in order to be of use to men, it must be relegated to a sphere where it can be of no use. You have no conception of the difficulty a careful reader has in knowing what you think, or what you mean. Sure it is that no human being can tell what you believe; but if your enunciations do not dance on the brink of Atheism, admit all its claims, then indeed Atheism is not. Such the is man who prates of God's Church being too sacred for a certain partnership. Whatever may be said of Mormonism, it is certain you would have to mend your theology before you could be admitted a member of that Church.

But you are not done with the subject yet. There are admissions, to be explained. You have already stated that the purity of the state depends on the purity of the Church. If the latter is corrupted the state also becomes corrupt. If, therefore, the perpetuity and morality of the state depend on the condition of the Church, then the Church is wholly indispensible to the state, for you have in effect, said the one depends upon the other. If you have not said this, then your words have no meaning. If, therefore, they be divorced, the state falls, for its moral, and necessarily therefore, its corporate existence, is due to the purity of the Church. Being no Church, there is for the State no anchor, no guide, no safeguard from destruction, and it must fall. This last is a

Christian principle, and you like it when it suits you; but when, to establish another point, you assert there can be no partnership between them, the Church is "too sacred," they must stand apart, you play the Atheist to his utmost bent. There is no basis on which to hang a man who holds first the State as dependent on the Church, and then declares they must be divorced for the benefit of the Church. The whole point and pith and purpose of your words go to show that the destruction of the Church is absolutely essential to the welfare of the State. How base and fallen is one that endeavors to hoodwink himself.

CHAPTER XIII.

TUCKER CONCLUDED.—WHAT IS IMMORALITY?—THE PRODI-
GAL'S RETURN.—COMPARISONS UNDESIRABLE.—SO MUCH
RISK FOR SO LITTLE AND THEN TO LOSE.—GOING OUT OF
PUBLIC LIFE.—A VAIN LIFE.—PITY FOR THE WEAK.—A
DAY SIGNALIZED.—BLESSED TIME.—TIME COMES WHEN
ALL IS FORGOTTEN.—WHERE MEN SHOULD DIE.—A
FINISHED TASK.—THE UNSEEN LINE.

TUCKER. What I want is that this Government shall set its face forever against this immorality. [Loud applause.] I believe to-day that with the passage of this bill, which is not unjust to any of them; and with the passage of the Constitutional amendment, which simply provides that the Territory, when it comes in, shall not go back on its record as an anti-polygamous Territory, and shall not "return as a dog to his vomit or a sow to her waller in the mire;" and that this crime of polygamy shall be a constiutional crime, just as treason is a constitutional crime; and that the punishment for polygamy shall be prescribed by Congress as is the punishment of treason, and shall be tried by the Federal courts just as treason is tried; that this evil will be forever stamped out.

COMMENT. What you want is the government forever, to set its face against this immorality? We have heard you make use of this language, within half an hour. "Why, sir, what is this Mormonism? *Is it merely polygamy?* Are we dealing here with the individual crime of the individual man? Not at all, or only incidentally. That is a *very small part of the whole business.*" Comment were painful. What can you think of yourself?

Many things are made crimes by the law which are not immoral; many things immoral which are not crimes. That is not necessarily immoral which is opposed to our senses or to our prejudices; nor is that always moral which pleases us most, or which our sentiment applauds. I mention this simply because you manifest a determined inclination to use the words as synonymous. That is immoral which is opposed to the law of God. Ignore them by the absence of laws as much as we choose, still those things remain immoral which are contrary to God's will. This is not the place to discuss the morality of polygamy or any of its features. But it is not sufficient for you to assert it to be immoral; nor to misapply and belie the Savior, as you have done, to maintain a shameful and slanderous positon. If it be a sin and immoral, it is so because God has so declared it to be. The ingenuity, cunning, legal lore, baseness, sophistry, falsehood and brains of all the quacks in politics that ever lived, backed up by laws and bills, mountains high and oceans wide, cannot make it a sin or immoral unless the Omnipotent Lawgiver has so declared it. This much may be said: You have not proven it to be immoral. Its results do not prove it to be such; nature does not condemn it, and where men denounce it the law of God is silent. And a further remark: If it be immoral, it is impure. Perhaps this nineteenth century Zeus will show where, in polygamous nations, exist the heinous crimes (abounding in monogamous and so-called Christian countries) which are the grief of all good men and women, of the heroic Tucker himself. Is there no purity of life among Musselmen? The comparison between their morality and our "plant of European-American growth" is one that no sane advocate of Christian and civilized monogamy will wisely invite. Ah me, how often do Goldsmith's words recur to the mind in this age. "Some men think they pay every debt to virtue by praising it."

Back again to polygamy and immorality—the last resort of demagogues and sycophantish purists, just as patriotism is the last cry of scoundrels. The church forgotten, its accumlations unminded, the divorcement of state and Church ignored. Back again to polygamy, and whip your little soul into a fury till your doting head shake, and your failing voice crack again. To stamp out polygamy! How many windings in behalf of this "job"—and that it should fail! What sacrifices of truth, honor, principle, of a life-long reputation, in the vain and futile hope of triumphing over a handful of poor, weak, powerless, almost friendless Mormons. Vain! vain! So much to risk for so little—and then to lose!

TUCKER. I feel a deep interest in the question, because, as I said a few weeks ago, I am going out of public life. If I can do anything to establish a pure system in that unfortunate Territory by uprooting this criminal institution of its society, which has been a foul blot upon the name and civilization of the whole country, and thus permit this Territory, when the proper time shall come, to enter into the pure sisterhood of States with the institution of a pure Christian home as the basis of its polity, then I shall feel that my humble public life has not been altogether in vain. [Prolonged applause.]

COMMENT. Has it not already been said: Whom the gods would destroy they first made mad? This the consummation of a life of public service! Arrayed with—nay, leading—a wild mob against a handful of helpless Mormons, helpless save for an unshaken trust in God. Against whom it is necessary to speak falsely to make a case. Relegated to private life with a falsehood on your lips and wild hatred in your heart—hatred of the defenseless, the industrious, the thrifty, the weak, of the earth against whom all men are massed. Trading on a reputation for intelligence, principle and veracity to secure the death of a system that has enriched the country, caused men to lead pious lives, and blossemed with a thousand virtues (admitting as true all that is said against it) that would grace the life and adorn the character of even a Tucker! It this be accomplished, "then I shall feel that my public life has not been altogether vain." "Vain otherwise?" asks the thoughtful reader. No, not vain. Results for good or evil are long enduring, but better vain than to succeed in that which can be secured by public clamor and unreason alone. But let us be just.

> "No one can ever truly see
> Another's highest, noblest part,
> Save through the sweet philosophy
> And loving wisdom of the heart."

When time shall have swept away the mists from before our eyes, and the hearts of men and their motives shall stand revealed, there may be in the life of J. Randolph Tucker that which will mitigate the abuse of power which Almighty God, in His economy, has permitted this man to use. Men who do wrong are to be pitied. Pity him. A strong man had been wiser; the weak claim our sympathy, though their arrogance often begets our contempt.

TUCKER. Let the evening of January 12th, be signalized by the passage of this bill.

COMMENT. How great a blessing is time! For with unerring tread she strides over the ephemeral and evanescent reputations of men, crushing, grinding, to dust, till all be lost and forgotten. Sweet oblivion! Sweetest of all to those who, having been given power of men, abuse that power! Even the 12th of January, 1887, will be forgotten. Time comes when this bill will be forgotten; when its successor will be no more; when the memory of it, its authors, advocates, executors, defenders, and assailants are no more. Could evil always live, could its effects be prolonged, wearing forever new vestures after the fashion of the old, there would come an hour, when the names that have plead for such measures as this, would be synonyms for all that is base, vile, cheap and corrupt. 'Twere better never to have been born, than be among those who force effects that for time and time, bring but evil to men. Ah, no! A friendly Providence has ordained that we often be saved from ourselves; and 'tis blessed so. But for the hereafter! The lies, sophistries, applause, pomp, power, reasonings of this life, of what avail then? Think of it, man! What answer will they make to Infinite Justice, when the last farth-

ing will be demanded? Wise men find in each day sufficient
for itself. And if for the future we build, if to have lived not
in vain, how shall we act? Better the humble walk in life, better a name unknown, a fame unsung, an unmarked grave, the
unread history of a life that was true, than all the praise, applause, power and pomp that cunning and lying, force from
the vanity of vain men and mad! Such a life works forever
for good. Its effect is for always! It has the blessed countenance of the Son of Righteousness.

> How little reeks it where men die,
>   When once the moment's past
> In which the dull and glazing eye
>   Has looked on earth its last?
>
> Whether, beneath the sculptured urn
>   The coffined form shall rest,
> Or, in its nakedness, return
>   Back to its mother's breast.
>
> Death is a common friend or foe,
>   As different men may hold,
> But, at its summons, each must go,
>   The timid and the bold;
>
> But when the spirit, free and warm,
>   Deserts us, as it must,
> What matter where the lifeless form
>   Resolves again to dust?
>
> 'Twere sweet, indeed, to breathe our last,
>   With those we cherish near,
> And, wafted upward by their sighs,
>   Soar to some calmer sphere.
>
> But whether on the gallows high,
>   Or in the battles' van,
> *The fittest place where man can die,*
>   IS WHERE HE DIES FOR MAN.

The task is done. It has grown beyond expectation. Legal
questions have not been touched. Much that might have been
said has been omitted. No defense of Mormon doctrines has

been attempted. The whole purpose has been, by the very speeches made in behalf of this measure, to demonstrate the intent as false, the reason spurious and destructively contradictory, and, on the very showing made by the advocates of the bill, to prove they had no case. I believe it has been done. The assertions made to bolster up the bill are contradictory and destructive of each other; they are false; the reasoning is spurious and vain, the intent not to affect polygamy but to destroy a church and bring a people into a political slavery. The measure was conceived in hatered, based on falsehood, born for robbery and spoliation, and fed by prejudice, ignorance and wickedness of heart.

How long will the people of this nation countenance such a course? What a tale ot duplicity, fraud, ignorance, imbecility, designed robbery and slavery, these speeches reveal when examined by the light of—yes, by the light only of a tallow dip. Let the wise pause. Let them ask: Are we deceived alone on this subject? Liars are always liars. Wise men trust them in nothing. There is a line. Citizen, voter, reader, man, has it not been reached?

> There is a time, we know not when,
>   A point, we know not where,
> That marks the destiny of men
>   To glory or dispair.
> There is a line, to us unseen,
>   That crosses every path,
> The hidden boundary between
>   God's mercy and His wrath.

TUCKER'S SUBSTITUTE.

FOLLOWING is the bill which Mr. Tucker reported as a substitute for the Senate bill, and which was under consideration at the time the speeches reviewed were delivered.

That in any proceedings and examination before a grand jury, a judge, justice, or a United States commissioner, or a court, in any prosecution for bigamy, polygamy, or unlawful cohabitation, under any statute of the United States, the lawful husband or wife of the person accused shall be a competent witness, and may be called, but shall not be compelled to testify in such proceeding, examination, or prosecution, and shall not be permitted to testify as to any statement or communication made by either husband or wife to each other, during the existence of the marriage relation, deemed confidential at common law.

SEC. 2. That in any prosecution for bigamy, polygamy or unlawful cohabitation, under any statute of the United States, whether before a United States commissioner, justice, judge, a grand jury, or any court, an attachment for any witness may be issued by the court, judge, or commissioner, without a previous subpœna, compelling the immediate attendance of such witness, when it shall appear, by the oath or affirmation of at least two credible persons in writing, to the commissioner, justice, judge, or court, as the case may be, that there is reasonable ground to believe that such witness will unlawfully fail to obey a subpœna issued and served in the usual course in such cases: and in such case the usual witness fees shall be paid to such witness so attached: *Provided*, That the person so attached may at any time secure his or her discharge from custody by executing a recognizance before any commissioner, judge, justice or court, of the United States, with sufficient surety, conditioned for the appearance of such person at the proper time as a witness in the cause or proceeding wherein the attachment may be issued.

SEC. 3. That every ceremony of marriage, or in the nature of a marriage ceremony, of any kind, in any of the Territories of the United States, whether either or both or more of the parties to such ceremony be lawfully competent to be the subjects of such marriage or ceremony, or not, shall be certified by a writing stating the fact and nature of such ceremony, the full name of each of the parties concerned, and the full name of every officer, priest, and person, by whatever style or designation called or known, in any way taking part in the performance of such ceremony, which certificate shall be drawn up and signed by the parties to such ceremony, and by every officer, priest, and person taking part in the performance of such ceremony, and shall be by the officer, priest, or other person solemnizing such marriage or ceremony filed in the office of the probate court, or, if there be none, in the office of the court having probate powers in the county or district in which such ceremony shall take place, for record, and shall be immediately recorded, and be at all times subject to inspection as other public records. Such certificate, or the record thereof, or a duly certified copy of such record, shall be *prima facie* evidence of the facts required by this act to be stated therein, in any proceeding, civil or criminal, in which the matter shall be drawn in question. Any person who shall wilfully violate any of the provisions of this section shall be deemed guilty of a misdemeanor, and shall on conviction thereof, be punished by a fine of not more than $1.000, or by imprisonment not longer than two years, or by both said punishment, in the discretion of the court.

SEC. 4. That nothing in this act shall be held to prevent the proof of marriages whether lawful or unlawful, by any evidence now legally admissible for that purpose,

SEC. 5. That it shall not be lawful for any female to vote at any election hereafter held in the Territory of Utah for any public purpose whatever, and no such vote shall be received or counted or given effect in any manner whatever; and any and every act of the governor and Legislative Assembly of the Territory of Utah providing for or allowing the registration or voting by females is hereby annulled.

SEC. 6. That all laws of the Legislative Assembly of the Territory of Utah which provide for numbering or identifying the votes of the electors at any election in said Territory are hereby disapproved and annulled; but the foregoing provision shall not preclude the lawful registration of voters, or any other provisions for securing fair elections which do not involve the disclosure of the canddiates for whom any particular elector shall have voted.

SEC. 7. That the laws enacted by the Legislative Assembly of the Territory of Utah conferring jurisdiction upon probate courts, or the judges thereof, or any of them, in said Territory, other than in respect of the estates of deceased persons, and in respect of the guardianship of the persons and property of infants, and in respect of the persons and property of persons not of sound mind, are hereby disapproved and annulled; and no probate court or judge of probate shall exercise any jurisdiction other than in respect of the matters aforesaid; and every such jurisdiction, so by force of this act withdrawn from the said probate courts or judges, shall be had and exercised by the district courts of said Territory, respectively.

SEC. 8. That if any person related to another person within and not including the fourth degree of consanguinity, computed according to the rules of the civil law, shall marry or cohabit with or have sexual intercourse with such other so related person, knowing him or her to be within said degree of relationship, the person so offending shall be deemed guilty of incest, and, on conviction thereof, shall be punished by imprisonment in the penitentiary not less than three years and not more than fifteen years.

SEC. 9. That when sexual intercourse is committed between a married person of one sex and an unmarried person of the other sex, both persons shall be deemed guilty of adultery, and shall, upon conviction thereof be punished by fine not exceeding $100, or by imprisonment not exceeding three months, or both, in the discretion of the court.

SEC. 10. That all laws of the Legislaitve Assembly of the Territory of Utah which provide that prosecutions for adultery can be commenced only on the complaint of the husband or wife are hereby disapproved and annulled; and all prosecutions for adultery may hereafter be instituted in the same way that prosecutions for other crimes are.

SEC. 11. That the marriage relation between one person of either sex and more than one person of the other sex shall be deemed polygamy. Polygamy or any polygamous association or cohabitation between the sexes is hereby declared to be a felony, and shall be punished by confinement in the penitentiary for a term not less than one year nor more than five years; and the continuance of the polygamy or polygamous association or cohabitation between the sexes after any indictment or other legal proceeding is commenced against any person shall be deemed a new offense, punishable as aforesaid.

SEC. 12. That the laws enacted by the Legislative Assembly of the Territory of Utah, which provide for or recognize the capacity of illegitimate children to inherit or be entitled to any distributive share in the estate of the father of such illegitimate child are hereby disapproved and annulled; and no illegitimate child shall hereafter be entitled to inherit from his or her father or to receive any distributive share of the estate of his or her father: *Provided*, That this section shall not apply to any illegitimate child born within twelve months after the passage of this act, nor to any child made legitimate by the seventh section of the act entitled "An act to amend section 5352 of the Revised Statutes of the United States, in reference to bigamy, and for other purposes," approved March 22, 1882.

SEC. 13. That nothing in this act contained shall be construed to repeal the act of Congress entitled, "An act to amend section 5352 of the Revised Statutes of the United States, in reference to bigamy, and for other purposes," approved March 22, 1882; but the provisions of said act, except in so far as they are repugnant to this act, shall be applicable to this act as if herein expressly mentioned; and the power given to the President by the sixth section of said act shall be applicable to the offenses created by this act.

SEC. 14. That the acts of the Legislative Assembly of Utah incorporating, continuing, or providing for the corporation known as the Church of Jesus Christ of Latter-day Saints, and the ordinance of the so-called general assembly of the state of Deseret incorporating the Church ot Jesus Christ of Latter-day Saints, so far as the same may now have legal force and validity, are hereby disapproved and annulled, and the said corporation, in so far as it may now have, or pretend to have, any legal existence, is hereby dissolved.

SEC. 15. That all laws of the Legislative Assembly of the Territory ot Utah, or of the so-called government of the state of Deseret, creating, organizing, amending, or continuing the corporation or association called the Perpetual Emigration Fund Company are hereby disapproved and annulled; and the said corporation, in so far as it may now have, or pretend to have, any legal existence, is hereby dissolved; and it shall not be lawful for the Legislative Assembly of the Territory of Utah to create, organize, or in any manner recognize any corporation or association, or to pass any law, for the purpose of or operating to accomplish the bringing of persons into the said Territory for any purpose whatsoever.

SEC. 16. That it shall be the duty of the Attorney-General of the United States to cause such proceedings to be taken in the supreme court of the Territory of Utah as shall be proper to declare void and to dissolve the said corporations mentioned in the preceding section and in the fourteenth section of this act, and pay the debts and to dispose of the property and assets thereof according to law and equity.

SEC. 17. That the eleventh paragraph of the third section of the act entitled "An act in relation to courts and judicial officers of the Territory of Utah," approved June 23, 1874, be, and the same is hereby, amended so as to read as follows:

"A writ of error from the Supreme Court of the United States to the supreme court of the said Territory shall lie in all criminal cases where the accused shall have been sentenced to capital punishment, or convicted of bigamy, polygamy, or unlawful cohabitation, or of any] offense under the act entitled 'An act to amend section 5352 of the Revised Statutes of the United States, in reference to bigamy, and for other purposes,' approved March 22, 1882, or under this act, whether the judgment complained of was rendered before or after the approval of this act; and a writ of error from the Supreme Court of the United States to the supreme court of the Territory, or an appeal to the Supreme Court of the United States from the supreme court of the Territory, shall likewise lie and be allowed as to any judgment or decree rendered in any proceeding or suit authorized under the sixteenth section of this act; and the Supreme Court of the United States is authorized to speed all cases arising under this section, and dispose of them as promptly as possible, without regard to place upon the docket: *Provided, however,* That the writ of error or appeal hereby allowed shall be taken and prosecuted within the period limited in like cases from judgments and decrees of the circuit courts of the United States, or within one year from the approval of this act."

SEC. 18. That all religious societies, sects, or denominations shall have the right to have and to hold, through trustees appointed by the several county courts of the Territory, so much real property for the erection of houses of worship, and for the residence of minister, priest, or other religious teacher, as shall be needed for the convenience and use of the several congregations of such religious society, sect or denomination: *Provided, however,* That such real property shall not exceed in an incorporated town or city ten acres, or elsewhere fifty acres; nor shall any such society, sect, or denomination have and hold, except in the value of buildings erected on said real property as aforesaid, and in the value of the personal property used in religious worship or for the comfort of those assembled therefor, a greater amount in money value than $50,000,

SEC. 19. That commissioners appointed by the supreme court and district courts in the Territory of Utah shall possess and may exercise all the powers and jurisdiction that are or may be possessed or exercised by justices of the peace in said Territory under the laws thereof, and the same powers conferred by law on commissioners appointed by circuit courts of the United States.

SEC. 20. That the marshal of said Territory of Utah, and his deputies, shall possess and may exercise all the powers in executing the laws of the United States possessed and exercised by sheriffs and their deputies as peace officers; and each of them shall arrest or cause to be arrested all offenders against the law in his view, and carry them before the proper officer or court for examination according to law. They shall have power to prevent assaults and batteries, and to quell and suppress riots, routs, and affrays.

SEC. 20. That all laws passed by the so-called state of Deseret and by the Territory of Utah for the organization of the militia thereof or for the creation of the Nauvoo legion are hereby annulled, repealed, and declared void and of no effect; and the militia of Utah shall be organized and subjected in all respects to the laws of the United States regulating the militia in the Territories: *Provided, however,* That all general officers of the militia shall be appointed by the governor of the Territory, by and with the advice and consent of the council thereof. The Legislative Assembly of Utah shall have power to pass laws for organizing the militia thereof, subject to the approval of Congress.

SEC. 21. That all laws passed by the general assembly of Deseret or by the Legislative Assembly of Utah granting or confirming any water, timber, or herd rights on any part of the public domain, or any special privilege therein, to any person or to any civil or ecclesiastical corporation or association, or to any person for the use and benefit of any such corporation or association, are hereby annulled and declared void; and the Attorney-General of the United States is hereby directed to cause such proceedings to be had in the supreme court of the Territory of Utah as shall enforce this section, and also to avoid and set aside all fraudulent entries upon homestead or pre-emption claims to lands in said Territory as may come to his knowledge; and the supreme court of said Territory shall have all needful jurisdiction in law and equity for the purposes of this act.

SEC. 22. (*a*) A widow shall be endowed of the third part of all the lands whereof her husband was seized of an estate of inheritance at any time during the marriage, unless she shall have lawfully released her right thereto.

(*b*) The widow of any alien who at the time of his death shall be entitled by law to hold any real estate, if she be an inhabitant of the Territory at the time of such death, shall be entitled to dower of such estate in the same manner as if such alien had been a native citizen.

(*c*) If a husband seized of an estate or inheritance in lands, exchanges them for other lands, his widow shall not have dower of both, but shall make her election to be endowed of the lands given or of those taken in exchange; and if such election be not evinced by the commencement of proceedings to recover her dower of the lands given in exchange within one year after the death of her husband, she shall be deemed to take her dower of the lands received in exchange.

(*d*) When a person seized of an estate of inheritance in lands shall have executed a mortgage or other like conveyance before marriage, his widow shall nevertheless be entitled to dower out of the lands mortgaged or so conveyed, as against every person except the mortgage or grantee and those claiming under him.

(*e*) Where a husband shall purchase lands during coverture, and shall at the same time execute a mortgage or other like conveyance of his estate in such lands to secure the payment of the purchase-money, his widow shall not be entitled to dower out of such lands, as against the mortgagee or other grantee, or those claiming under him, although she shall not have united in such mortgage; but she shall be entitled to her dower in such lands as against all other persons.

(*f*) Where in such case the mortgagee or other grantee, or those claiming under him, shall, after the death of the husband of such widow, cause the land mortgaged or so conveyed to be sold, either under a power of sale contained in the mortgage or conveyence or by virtue of the decree of a court of equity, and if any surplus shall remain after payment of the moneys due on such mortgage or conveyance, and the costs and charges of the sale, such widow shall nevertheless be entitled to the interest or income of the one-third part of such surplus for her life as her dower.

(*g*) A widow shall not be endowed of lands conveyed to her husband by way of mortgage unless he acquire an absolute estate therein during the marriage period.

(*h*) In case of divorce dissolving the marriage contract for the misconduct of the wife, she shall not be endowed.

(*i*) The term "lawful wife," wherever used in this statute, shall be held to mean, in all cases of Mormon or plural marriages, the first wife; and such wife only shall be entitled to dower under this act on the death of her husband.

SEC. 23. That the existing election districts and apportionments of representation concerning the members of the Legislative Assembly of the Territory of Utah are hereby abolished; and it shall be the duty of the governor, Territorial secretary, and the United States marshal in said Territory forthwith to redistrict said Territory, and apportion representation in the same in such manner as to provide, as nearly as may be, for an equal representation of the people (excepting Indians not taxed), being citizens of the United States, according to numbers, in said Legislative Assembly, and to the number of members of the council and house of representatives, respectively, as now established by law; and a record of the establishment of such new districts and the apportionment of representation thereto shall be made in the office of the secretary of said Territory, and such establishment and representation shall continue until Congress shall otherwise provide; and no persons other than citizens of the United States otherwise qualified shall be entitled to vote at any election in said Territory.

SEC. 24. That the provisions of section 9 of said act, approved March 22, 1882, in regard to registration and election officers, and the registration of voters, and the conduct of elections, and the powers and duties of the board therein mentioned, shall continue and remain operative until the provision and laws therein referred to, to be made and enacted by the Legislative Assembly of said Territory of Utah, shall have been made and enacted by said assembly and shall have been approved by Congress.

SEC. 25. That every male person over twenty-one years of age resident in the Territory of Utah shall appear before the clerk of the probate court of the county wherein he resides, and register himself by his full name, with his age, place of business, his status, whether single or married, and if married, the name of his lawful wife, and shall take and subscribe an oath, to be filed in said court, stating the facts aforesaid, and that he will support the Constitution of the United States and will faithfully obey the laws thereof, and especially will obey the law aforesaid approved March 22, 1882, and this act, in respect of the crimes in said acts defined and forbidden; and that he will not directly or indirectly aid, abet, counsel, or advise, any other person to commit the same. No person not so registered, or who shall have been convicted of any crime under this act or under "An act to amend section 5352 of the Revised Statutes of the United States, in reference to bigamy, and for other purposes," approved March 22, 1882, or who shall be a polygamist, or associate or cohabit polygamously with persons of the other sex, or who shall not take and subscribe the oath aforesaid, shall be entitled to vote in any election in the Territory, or be capable of jury service, or to hold any office of trust or emolument in the Territory.

SEC. 26. That the council of the Territory of Utah shall hereafter consist of thirteen members, appointed by the President, by and with the advice and consent of the Senate, every two years, the members of which shall be citizens resident in the said Territory, one to be selected from each district of the Territory, according to the apportionment provided for in the twenty-third section of this act.

SEC. 27. That all judges of the county and probate courts and selectmen of each county of said Territory, and all clerks of said courts, justices of the peace, sheriffs, constables, and other Territorial, county, and district officers, shall (after the expiration of the terms of office of those now in office) be appointed as follows: and all laws to the contrary are hereby repealed:

The President shall have power to nominate and, by and with the advice and consent of the Senate, to appoint all judges and selectmen of the county and probate courts for the term of two years. The said courts shall appoint their clerks, recorders, and registers of deeds, wills, and other papers by law required to be recorded.

The governor, by and with the advice and consent of the council, shall have power to appoint all justices of the peace, all sheriffs, constables, and other county and district officers, and all other officers of the Territory not herein otherwise provided for.

SEC. 28. That the office of Territorial superintendent of district schools created by the laws of Utah is hereby abolished; and it shall be the duty of the governor of said Territory to appoint a commissioner of schools, who shall possess and exercise all the powers and duties heretofore imposed by the laws of said Territory upon the Territorial superintendent of district schools, and who shall receive the same salary and compensation, which shall be paid out of the treasury of said Territory. The said commissioner shall have power to prohibit the use in any district school of any book of a sectarian character or otherwise unsuitable. Said commissioner shall collect and classify statistics and other information respecting the district schools in said Territory, showing their progress, the whole number of children of school age, the number who attend school in each year in the respective counties and average length of time of their attendance, the number of teachers, and the compensation paid to the same, the number of teachers who are Mormons, the number who are not Mormons, the number of children of Mormon parents, and the number of children of parents who are not Mormons, and their respective average attendance at school. All of which statistics and information shall be annually reported to Congress through the governor of said Territory and the Department of the Interior.

www.ingramcontent.com/pod-product-compliance
Lightning Source LLC
Chambersburg PA
CBHW030547270326
41927CB00008B/1545